# LEARNING FOR LIFE

# Mowbray Parish Handbooks

# LEARNING FOR LIFE

## A HANDBOOK OF ADULT RELIGIOUS EDUCATION

Yvonne Craig

MOWBRAY

**Mowbray**
A Cassell imprint
Villiers House, 41/47 Strand, London WC2N 5JE
387 Park Avenue South, New York 10016–8810

First published 1994

British Library Cataloguing-in-Publication Data
A catalogue record for this book is available from the British Library.

Library of Congress Cataloging-in-Publication Data
Applied for.

ISBN 0–264–67318–2

Typeset by Intype, London
Printed and bound in Great Britain by
Biddles Ltd, Guildford and King's Lynn

# Contents

# Foreword

Life is an exploration and an adventure. The only people who are old are those who think they have learnt all they need to know and have given up discovering. For the rest of us each day reminds us of our ignorance and needles us towards discovering more, both about ourselves and about life and faith. As the years take their toll and our minds become less nimble and our memories more perforated, we need a surer understanding of why we find it more difficult to learn and how we can discover new ways of learning and exploring. This books opens our minds to the art of learning and unlearning and yet does not despise techniques and practicalities. Yvonne Craig, writing from her own experience and with a vast knowledge of adult educational method, makes us feel young again through the wisdom and humour of this book.

✠ *MICHAEL GUILDFORD*

# Introduction

*Learning for Life* can be used in several ways. Some may read it straight through. Others may start by discovering their own preferred learning style (Chapter 4) and then select what they need. Pragmatists may find Chapters 5, 6 and 7 particularly useful. Those who enjoy reflection and theory-tasting are likely to warm to the first three chapters plus 7 and 8. Chapters 5, 6 and 9 stand in their own right to be dipped into when needed. They may be specially useful for those activitists who learn best on the job.

Chapter 1 starts with a list of the many signs of hope which changing circumstances are bringing.

Chapter 2 explains and illustrates six different models of adult religious education, each with particular strengths and limitations. It offers ways of working out which of them will be most fruitful in your circumstances, having first raised a number of theological issues you need to be clear about since often our taken-for-granted assumptions mould what we do.

Chapter 3 lists factors which help adults to learn and confronts some of the inaccurate things people say about our learning capacity.

Chapter 4 describes the learning cycle and offers a questionnaire to help you detect your own preferred learning style so that, aware of the range of possibilities, you can reflect on the link between your experience as a learner and your strengths as an educator.

Chapter 5 describes, page by page with examples, 25 methods which adult educators and trainers use, together with the specific usefulness and weakness of each.

Chapter 6 offers a way of putting all these things together in a section on planning educational events.

Chapter 7 is a brief introduction to some of the hidden factors at work when groups meet and contains a section on group leadership.

Chapter 8 tackles the thorny issue of assessment and accreditation, against a background of changes in the national system which are already beginning to affect the Church. It also contains a brief glossary of terms which may be unfamiliar to some.

Chapter 9 describes nine real-life events which illustrate some of the ideas in this book, together with comments on their usefulness by the people who ran them.

# Acknowledgements

I would like to thank the following friends and colleagues, all training and educational professionals, from whom I have obtained ideas, advice and examples, especially Andrew Aldrich, Michael Allen, Paul Bates, Anton Baumohl, Anthony Clarke, Sue Cumming, Anne Horton, Walter James, Ian Knox, Celia Leam, Paul Mortimore, Terry Oakley, Wendy Robins, Roger Walton and others mentioned in the text.

I would also like to thank Richard Craig, Hilary Ineson, Sheila Green, Keith Lamdin, Ann Murch and Laurence Reading, without whose generous gift of time and encouragement this book would never have been written.

# 1

# New Challenge and New Hope

The Archbishop of Canterbury spoke recently of 'the splendid wilderness of the world' we are called to engage with.

> The church is waking up to the fact that its task is too big and too important to be left in the hands of the few, when set against the needs of to-day's world . . .
> . . . A Copernican vision is required of us to see at the centre of God's mission not the splendid work of church life but the equally splendid wilderness of the world – where there are few places for Christians to hide, where moral or ethical signposts are blurred or non-existent and where we are outnumbered by the indifferent, the unholy and the uncultured despisers of our day . . .
> . . . It will require a radical change of attitude from us all. It will mean being prepared not to jettison all that we have for the sake of something new and different but of humbly accepting that the local church must come second to the needs of those serving Christ in the world and the real needs of the communities in which we live.

What does this mean for those of us who want to help others grow in faith?

## In 'the splendid wilderness of the world . . .'

*Learning as an adult is no longer an optional extra for the curious or adventurous*

The old days of going to school or Sunday School to receive a lump sum of learning which you had to eke out for the rest of your life are over. Education means spending a lifetime learning how to gain knowledge and use it wisely. A new phrase which has crept into the literature is 'enterprise learning'. We are expected to pick up new techniques and information simply to run our daily lives. Perhaps decimalization of the coinage is the watershed which some of us remember. In recent years many of us have learned to travel abroad, cook new foods, cope with unprecedented family arrangements, work new machines (many people are surprised to discover they have 20 or 30 electric motors in home and garden, counting the last discarded Walkman, razor and hair dryer).

In addition, more people have free time. There are chilling reasons for this like unemployment and heartening reasons like living longer. Some say that there are school-leavers who will never be offered paid employment. What most men and women can look forward to is a lifetime of adjustment: paid work outside or inside the home, part-time or full-time, interspersed with unpaid work in the home or the community.

More and more people are spending that free time on learning. They buy or borrow car maintenance books, dress-making patterns, language tapes, watch or listen to documentaries, read specialist magazines on angling, photography, computing, parenting or how to make a poster.

One in ten joins some kind of course. There are now for the first time ever more adult students on Further and Higher Education courses than young people. Adult education includes keep-fit for the elderly, a chance to learn to read or write, training to be a Reader, an Open University course for prison inmates. In other words, the tide of social attitudes is flowing with those who want to know, both inside and outside the Church.

Meanwhile the Church is seeing the importance of having an informed and articulate membership:

- Church leaders constantly go on record saying that the formation of all God's people is a top priority. In recent years there have been a number of major reports from different denominations saying the same thing.
- The number of people appointed with special responsibility in this area has increased rapidly in the last ten years. Some have parish, deanery, archdeaconry or diocesan charge. More and more are benefiting from

courses and qualifications offered by churches, universities, colleges and training institutes.

- There has also been a remarkable expansion of training work by individuals and organizations not directly sponsored by the mainstream Churches. New groups have established themselves in clearly targeted areas and long-established organizations have switched resources to build up training units. Some are customer-led in terms of finance. Some receive financial backing from other sources.

- Established centres such as Church colleges of Higher Education, theological colleges and courses now not only train teachers and clergy but prepare people for a wide range of ministry, paid and unpaid.

- National ecumenical Lent courses reach many people both within and without the Church.

- More resources than ever before are being produced: books, study guides, videos, tapes, packs, portfolios, etc.

- The Churches have been involved with local radio and other media opportunities and are now responding to the challenges of new legislation.

- There is an emphasis in the Decade of Evangelism on nurture and training.

- More and more people are going on retreat.

*Uncertainty is faced head on and even enjoyed*

'The certainties of one age are the problems of the next.'

A true story is told by a post-doctoral student who worked in the Cavendish Laboratory at Cambridge many years ago where in a decade there were ten Nobel prizewinners. On Wednesday afternoons everyone met, staff and students. The membership of the group and the task they had was founded on a single question: 'What is going wrong with my research?' These Nobel prizewinners had found a profoundly impressive technique to help them to learn: they confessed and bartered their ignorance.

Christians can become nervous at the prospect of uncertainty. None of us finds it easy. We are used to books by experts with whom we can agree or disagree but at least we know where they stand. But it becomes more difficult to proclaim overarching theories and universal guiding principles. We know how partial, limited and relative our knowledge is. We are more humble, less willing to make sweeping claims.

This applies to adult religious education as to anything else. There will be a lot of ideas in this book, ideas always checked out by values and practice:

- four styles of learning
- six models of education
- ten ways in which adults learn
- nine examples of good practice
- 25 methods to choose from . . .

You will be invited to pick your way through them and make decisions. It is a different way of working from:

- relying on an external expert to tell you what to do;
- attending a course which makes extravagant claims as to what it can do for you;
- appointing a trouble-shooter (person or committee) to sort it all out.

It means setting up a conversation between yourself and those you work with or have responsibility for in order to identify problem areas and opportunities, imagine ways ahead, work towards improvement and evaluate what happens.

Some people may initially feel this is all too much. It can be uncomfortable living in a world of tentative, provisional, contextual claims. But this is the world in which we live. Let us splash about and enjoy the untidiness and surprise of it all!

The late Bishop John Tinsley put it like this:

> We ought to be good at handling tentativeness with a sure hand and steady nerve because our title deeds are those of a people on the move who have no abiding city, who can go out in faith and who can live with change and more change without falling into despair.

*People seek to go beyond rationalism: the question 'What is knowledge?' is asked*

The Enlightenment tried to improve life by heroic human effort, through science and through rational forms of social organization and education which it was hoped would release human potential, increasing understanding, morality, justice and happiness. It has not quite worked out like that. 'Objectivity' is suspect. The poetic, mythic, irrational and imaginative are being reinstated. 'Science and philosophy must jettison their grandiose metaphysical claims and view themselves more modestly as just another set of narratives.'

The re-writing of what constitutes 'knowledge' is illustrated from science itself. Mary Anning was an ill-educated, provincial woman who discovered and rescued the remains of dinosaurs as they were exposed in the cliffs of Lyme Regis by the storms of the early nineteenth century. Without her scientific interest, business acumen and astonishing craftsmanship our knowledge of such creatures would be much less and half the museums of the world would be deprived of their most prized exhibits. Yet she received little credit in her own day. The contribution of a non-academic, locally-based craftswoman of genius is now recognized by the good and the great although it falls outside what was previously counted as serious science.

The boundaries between what is counted as real knowledge and what is not are changing. For a long time 'practical' or 'pastoral' theology was seen as a soft option, not to be compared with systematics or doctrine. It mirrored the sciences, where pure physicists looked down on a descending order: geophysicists, chemists, biochemists, biologists – social and human sciences were off the map! Now there is a new graciousness and recognition that human experience is many-faceted, that the old hierarchies have failed and that adult religious education is free to be more inclusive and thus richer.

It means fewer certainties. We ask questions about what is to be passed on by whom, when and in what manner. For example, instead of offering a fixed course of a predetermined length at a particular place which the student is free to join or not, we switch our attention to the learner. Increasingly what we offer is centred on the individual's needs. We affirm cultural, class and gender diversity and try to be flexible, responsive, even biddable. The course itself may be episodic and fragmented, fitting in the particular need. All is based on consent, negotiated and democratic.

This has not made things easier for those who teach. The new approach takes time, energy and imagination in a way that teaching a fixed course does not. But it honours the divine spark in each individual whom God has created and loves. If Church history, indeed the doctrine we teach, is in effect the experience and understanding of Christians from past centuries, our incarnational theology bids us attend to the experience and developing understanding of adult learners as qualitatively similar.

These new and more inclusive ways of looking at things have unleashed a powerful creativity. Doors have opened which remained shut for centuries. New experiences have transformed old ways of looking at things. In theology this has meant that those who were previously silent are encouraged to describe their vision. In the past those in authority forgot who was left out when telling a story and forgot the community basis of Scripture.

And there has been a price to pay. It is possible to be too pragmatic, too shallow, too dispersed. When differences among people and countries mean that ideas and institutions live alongside each other, each jostles for a place. Instead of a smooth, integrated pyramid, there is a noisy bustling marketplace. And ideas which used to percolate down or radiate up now also spread from side to side.

*The splendour of the here and now (and by implication the immanence of God) is valued*

'The wonderful wilderness' says 'yes' to what is before us, life in all its contingencies. It refuses to shape and squeeze the world to fit a theory, like an Ugly Sister who cuts off her heel so that she can wear the slipper that rightly belongs to Cinderella. Is not this at the heart of an incarnational religion?

*People not systems are important*

Robert Waddington, a former General Secretary of the Board of Education, tells this story:

Aunt Agatha lived in Bagshot, near Woking
  she had travelled in India
    had ashtrays made out of elephants' feet
      and you tripped over her tiger skin rugs.
She was a bridge player and collected a few dignified ladies to play in
her lounge
  the stake was 2p a rubber and they
    kept their hats on as they were not staying
      but going home soon to get hubbies' tea
        the loser made the tea.
One day a Littlewoods' pools winner arrived in Bagshot
  she came to play bridge in a trouser suit
    she wore large dangly ear-rings
      she flashed around £1 notes and she
        asked for a gin and tonic in the tea break
          and wore no hat.
Aunt Agatha said 'It is time to write down our rules on a card:
  Ladies will wear hats
  2p a rubber
  Losers make tea etc.'

The crisis came when a 'disconfirming other' appeared. What happens when disconcerting problems and paradoxes come along? We have to make sense of them, otherwise our cultural systems would be implausible. Ideology (including theology) assures a group it is right to be what it is and to do what it does. Without that assurance, the group would be ineffective.

But once the rule card is produced it has a dramatic effect. A community with an identity and dynamic of its own has thrown up a piece of knowledge and it works back at them. They seem to forget they have made it and it becomes hard to change. Some poor lady cannot afford a hat and with genuine pain Aunt Agatha says 'I'm so sorry, it says here "Ladies will wear hats". We'd like to bend the rules of course ... You must first purchase the rule card, understand the rules, be willing to obey them – and then you may come to the table.'

We now know as never before how questionable are the systems we construct. The events of 1989 in Europe have been compared in significance to the French Revolution and even the Reformation. They signify for the first time ever the recognition by the leaders of an ideocracy that their ideology has failed ... Marxism, Communism, Nazism, Capitalism, Socialism.

The new task is coping with the co-existence of many

human stories rather than any one grand scheme of things. It needs listening, understanding and silence, giving people the benefit of the doubt, if possible seeing them as allies. Another way of putting this is to say that 'the wonderful wilderness' invites us to see life as a 'happening' rather than a finished work of art. It may mean surprises. It may be incoherent. That is felt to be no bad thing.

## Play is valued

Life is laid-back, relaxed, playful. It doesn't take itself too seriously. Its 'I'm able to take it or leave it' attitude reminds us of an old-fashioned virtue – temperance – which enjoys pleasure but is not obsessed by it. Moreover by prudent attention to the rhythms of our body and nature, our decisions will spring out of our whole self and not the merciless push of a grinding will.

Sometimes we get carried away by the fun: each specialization develops its own language and to the outsider it sounds like a local dialect. Theology is no exception: it needs its own words to describe unique insights. But it can become an intellectual game whereby the player best able to produce patterns pleasing to other players wins. The new player able to be pleased by the patterns produced by the leading players advances rapidly. The ball is picked up where the last player left it and play goes on. By this time there may be very few spectators left to be interested in the outcome.

In conclusion, Phillipa Berry, Fellow of King's College, Cambridge, wrote in the *Times Higher Educational Supplement:*

> [There is] a significant revival of interest in religion in certain sections of Western society ... this ... is not a simple return to an older form of religiosity but a much more complicated and tentative attempt to ... articulate a new model of the sacred. It is marked ... by intellectual reticence, by indirectness and irony. Nonetheless, it seems certain that the question of the sacred will be a vital part of the intellectual agenda of the 1990s.

*In this 'wonderful wilderness', what is the place of adult religious education?*

It is a truth universally acknowledged that the Christian faith was passed from generation to generation for nearly

2,000 years without anyone having heard the words 'adult education'. Stories were told, the New Testament written, creeds shaped, pictures painted, wood carved, dogmas hammered out, martyrs burned, psalms and hymns sung, sermons delivered. People learned about their faith from all these events.

Even today there are those who remind us not to get too carried away with an unhealthy regard for professionalism and techniques.

> The gifts of the Spirit are given, not learned. There have been myriads of people of deep wisdom and spiritual insight before the day of training courses . . . the formation of Christians is carried on in a million different ways. It does not hang upon the achievement of certificates or Church appointments.

But it is also true that over the centuries certain people set aside their time to teach others the faith in a systematic way. Religious communities (clerical and lay), universities, colleges and schools were founded. Householders instructed their servants, mothers taught their children the catechism, people painted the whole Bible systematically on church walls, missionaries organized classes for those who had never heard the Gospel. Methodism brought Bible classes to Cornish miners.

*Adult religious education is 'the planned effort to provide opportunities to enable adults to awake or deepen the knowledge, understanding and daily living of their faith' (Getting Started in Adult Religious Education, James De Boy (Paulist Press, 1979)).*

It believes

- God's love reaches out to all people, whether they are aware of it nor not, whether they respond to it or not.
- Nothing we do is exempt from the claims of the gospel or the intelligent, sensitive application of Christian thinking and learning to it.
- Most Christians are called 'to live fully in the secular world, to be at ease with it, to know its idioms and assumptions, to engage in its arguments and affairs . . . to be committed to them; and there in that place, where one's energies are committed, to engage quite consciously in mission and ministry'.
- The believing adult is often the only one who can

9

introduce the leaven of the kingdom, express the novelty and beauty of the gospel and demonstrate the will for liberation and change demonstrated by Jesus Christ.

It is against this rich and varied background that the next chapter invites you to examine what you think and believe about adult religious education and to appraise the consequences which flow from your beliefs.

# 2

# Choosing Between the Good and ... the Good

This chapter is in three sections:

A. *Theories at work*
Theories are not optional extras – everything we do as educators is based on them. An examination of some educational and theological assumptions.

B. *Six good ways of working:*

*Liberal education*
*Progressive education*
*Humanistic education*
*Technological education*
*Radical education*
*Dogmatic education*

An account of each one's values, processes, key words and particular strengths and limitations.

C. *A quiz*

## A. *Theories at work*

Our theological assumptions strongly influence not only the *content* but also the *way* we lead, teach, support, guide, advise and facilitate. Our educational plans, programmes and priorities mean that our theology is set out for all to see. No educational practice is neutral and if we change what we do it needs thinking through.

**What are the theological questions we must ask ourselves?
How will they affect what we do in teaching and learning?**

*A key question is: who or what is trustworthy?*

- Should we design educational programmes which control and protect students as we lead them to a saving knowledge of the truth? Or do we allow a great deal of freedom in the belief that our students have God-given curiosity, ability to think, concern for the well-being of others and a tendency towards just and loving behaviour?

- Can people be trusted to take the initiative because their hearts are restless until they find their rest in God or do they need sanctions and promises – sticks and carrots – to get them to learn?

- How is God most likely to be disclosed to us – in a theological treatise? in worship? in silence? in spirited discussion? in an act of service to the community?

- Do we train adults to take up responsibilities and roles in the Church as it is or do we encourage gifts which may be used to challenge established authority, question dogmas and chart new lands?

- How far do we teach about Christ through the Bible, theology, Church history and the writings of the saints who have gone before and how far is it a matter of helping others to enter redemptive experiences through just relationships, taking risks and sharing the spirit of Christ in a caring community?

- Is the Church an ark of salvation or a mission station in and to the world? Is it where the saved are nurtured or should it form servants who will stand alongside the poor and the oppressed?

- God has given the Church various ministries for equipping the saints for work in his service. How much of this is confined to the ordained ministry? or the accredited ministry? Who should do the teaching and guiding? Can I learn from a child or any ill-educated old person?

- Finally, are we talking about individuals each pursuing their own path towards the truth and Christian maturity? Or do we believe that Christian education, pastoral care and pastoral discipline are closely interwoven? 'Bonded and held together by every constituent joint, the whole frame grows through the proper functioning of each part, and builds itself up in love.'

There remains one final aspect of trust – the teacher/student relationship. All teachers would acknowledge that teaching and learning involve a delicate human transaction needing skill and sensitivity. Human beings are flawed and in our quest for truth we have mixed motives. It is always a precarious relationship because of:

- the anxieties of the learner about the threat of the teacher as judge and expert who might unmask us;
- the mixed feelings of the student who has to become to some extent dependent and lose some control;
- the teacher's own needs and motivations – to influence and control people and keep them dependent.

In a Christian learning situation students and teachers will bring assumptions based on their reading of Scripture and especially of the methods and attitudes of Jesus in the Gospels. Jesus taught the people with authority. The spectrum of trustworthiness is mirrored by the spectrum of authority. 'Who and what can I trust?' is a question which always involves some degree of submission to authority.

Saul Alinsky, the radical educationalist, remarked that people react to life as 'a series of happenings which pass through their systems undigested'. To help the digestive process we might describe what we do as: tutoring, guiding, supporting, instructing, 'enthusing' or teaching. What we choose to do is far more than a matter of selecting a personal style. In this chapter six different approaches will be described but they do not hang from a clothes rack waiting for us to choose the one that suits us best. Each is based on a view of what the world urgently needs and therefore what education is about. Each is limited in what it can do. Each of them is excellent in its own way.

But we cannot do everything. In practice we have to choose between the good and the good. Some things we need to leave to 'sanctified neglect', knowing that we leave undone those things which we might well have done and which other people are urging us to do.

**B.** *Six good ways of working: liberal, progressive, humanistic, technological, radical and dogmatic*

As you read, you may like to pause and consider your own past experience as a learner: what are you grateful for and what was downright restricting or misleading? Be as specific as your memory will allow, recalling people, events and places. Who or what really helped you? Perhaps you might like to give each model marks out of ten.

Then, consider which of the six models you normally use, or would like to use. You will find that you use more than one.

There may be another question: do people and things outside conspire to take you where you would rather not go? Ask yourself: is this the way I really want to work? If it is, what help do I need in order to do it even better? If it is not, does this mean that what I believe about education (espoused theory) and what I do (theory in practice) are very different? If so, is there anything I can do to bring them closer together? Give each model a different set of marks out of ten for usefulness in your present situation. But try to give them all the benefit of the doubt in some respects.

**Liberal education**

What do these events have in common?

- C. S. Lewis lecturing for an hour on one word: 'nature'.
- An ecumenical house group whose members in turn describe some distinguishing marks of their denomination's beliefs and practice.
- A tutor on a Bishop's Certificate Course giving a painstaking account of life in England under Mary Tudor.
- A packed church hall presided over by the local vicar with a panel of local people. The purpose is to advise the council on the best way of using a parcel of derelict land in the parish: a car park for local shops, a patch of green with flowers and a bench, or a small fenced all-weather games pitch?
- A careful account of some aspect of genetic engineering followed by two speakers with opposing views on what

control society should insist on, either through the law or voluntary codes of practice.

All these events can be described as liberal education. Liberal education is fashionable in some quarters but despised in others. For some people it is an idea which was tried but simply did not work. For others it is always élitist and exclusive. But before its undoubted weaknesses are put under the microscope, what are its special characteristics?

*The liberal educator believes that . . .*

**. . . *the most serious problem is* ignorance.** The liberal tradition began to have an impact on public education early this century and was pursued by people deeply committed to social and political reform. Great hopes were vested in what would happen to the nation and to individuals if they were better educated.

**. . . *the role of the educator is* transmission.** Teachers are custodians of treasures from the past and the present. They select what is valuable and their role is to pass it on to the student.

**. . . *what really counts as 'knowledge' is* wisdom.** The educated person not only gathers information and understanding but grows wiser, with sound moral values, a spiritual and religious dimension to life as well as an aesthetic sense. With a strong conviction of the importance of individual autonomy goes individual responsibility for the consequences of one's actions.

**. . . *education works by a process of* initiation** – into established forms of knowledge by those who know about such things.

**. . . *the key value is* reason.** This means that it is possible to be wrong. Any claim may be mistaken or false and need to be updated in the light of new evidence in a world in which intelligent beings are anything less than omniscient. So there is a search for impartial and unbiased criteria and standards of evidence in weighing up claims to knowledge. This is of course only defensible if you believe in objective truth. There is also a commitment to *freedom* which includes tolerating other people's claims to knowledge. This means a degree of pluralism.

... *the educated person is described as* 'knowledgeable'. Liberal education rests on a belief that greater understanding and knowledge of the universe and our place within it will of itself bring about a better world. 'The essential achievement of the will ... is to attend to a difficult object and hold it fast before the mind ... To sustain a representation, to think, is, in short, the only moral act...' (William James).

*What do its supporters say?*

Liberal education is so much part of our thinking that it is rarely discussed but it enshrines some values which are worth fighting for. Most of the readers of this book will have been shaped by it. It has underpinned our idea of a university, now currently living through a whirlwind of change.

The liberal educator –

– respects the individual and tries to give tools to help make sense of life experience. Is spacious and tolerant.
– seeks the truth. In instructing someone on a controversial issue, tries to be fair and balanced. But at its best does that not from a no-man's-land which does not belong to anyone, but from ground held with conviction. Is not anarchic. Reflects something of the God of truth and justice.
– does not make rash claims. Again at its best shows a fitting humility. Knows the limitations of human knowledge and does not pretend that we are anything other than finite creatures with partial knowledge. This resonates with a Christian acknowledgement of what is possible in a redeemed, but fallen, world.
– seeks the best. Uses the creation as a mirror which reflects something of God's image and celebrates it. Is enthusiastic about excellence, seeks it out wherever it may be, in the past and the present, in the acclaimed and the hidden places. Is not frightened by what it

might find. Christians rest assured in the belief that there is only one truth, God's truth, which cannot contradict itself.

– can live with ambiguity, mystery and surprise. In the current climate in education and training may have to take a firm stand on the belief that not everything can be measured.

– allows pluralism. Within its spacious walls, other approaches to education, fruitful in a different way, can flourish. Is it like a capacious mother, tolerant, tough, able to accept its offspring who are critical and creative?

### What are the weaknesses of **liberal** education?

Currently liberal education is suspect and this is what some of its critics say:

– It is too exclusive. For a start it depends on an ability to grasp concepts and make patterns with ideas, a gift not given to everyone. Not everyone can be an intellectual. George Steiner may well describe a classic as 'a book that will be a little newer the day after tomorrow than it will be tomorrow', but for some people tomorrow never comes.

– It is too bookish, assuming that learning from books gives you 'real' knowledge – everything else is second-class. This despite the fact that Christian faith through the centuries was usually passed on by word of mouth, often in the home by relations and servants. Many were women and most, until the last hundred or so years, were illiterate.

– It claims to be neutral but never can be. The very idea of objective knowledge is contentious. We know knowledge is never value-free or neutral. We may 'put both sides of the argument' but each of these is underpinned by so many taken-for-granted assumptions. Church history is a good example of the difficulties because it is the faith story of groups of people. How you tell it depends on where you stand and in any case we have to rely on written records and artifacts made by a tiny minority of the population. We know that history, like beauty, is in the eye of the beholder.

- The learner's experience is ignored. The idea of the adult Christian as an empty vessel to be filled by an expert will not do. The Christian community can be damaged and divided if useful knowledge is conveyed in a way which undermines it. Too often lay people, asked about a sermon, say 'I don't know enough about it to comment' because they do not know the value of their personal faith. And it can go badly wrong. It was Paul Tillich who said 'the fatal pedagogical error is to throw answers like stones at the heads of those who have not yet asked the questions'.
- It ignores human nature. It is unrealistic about what changes people's hearts and actions. It does not take sin seriously. Exposure to great minds through literature, theology, works of art, etc. is not enough – Germans who read Goethe and listened to Beethoven also ran concentration camps.
- It is too vague and woolly. It will not set limits. If the devil himself came along, would he be welcomed as presenting an interesting new aspect of the situation instead of being roundly condemned?
- It cannot be measured. How do you ever know that people have become 'wiser' for example? The Maze prison near Belfast is said to have the best educational record of any UK jail, largely because of the IRA prisoners who take A levels and Open University degrees in political studies. How can you measure outcomes?
- It is too rational. It takes you so far down a path of enlightenment but it backs away when presented by a faith statement. What use is this in religious education?

**Progressive education**

Possible scenarios:

- A national educational campaign to Keep Sunday Special.
- Lobbying the clergy team and members of the PCC which results in the use of the church hall for a mother-and-toddler club.
- A letter to those in charge of the diocesan training scheme for new churchwardens carefully setting out

the case for including a section on conservation in the churchyard.

These are all examples of progressive education. Sometimes they are a reaction against liberal trends by people who are impatient to change the world and the people in it.

*The progressive educator believes that . . .*

*. . . the most serious problem is how to bring about* **social and individual change.** It starts from a committed position. It wants to influence and change people in a certain direction. For some people this hardly counts as education at all.

*. . . the role of the educator is* **guidance.** There is a goal in view which both teacher and learner want to reach, probably after the latter has been persuaded. The teacher probably has more experience or information. But the way ahead is suggested not prescribed. And part of the process is not only overcoming a specific problem, but learning how to solve problems so that the process can be transferred and used elsewhere.

*. . . what really counts as knowledge is* **judgement and the ability to act.** Knowledge is not valued for its own sake but only in so far as it is lived out. Life experience is welcomed and shared. It can be as valuable as anything stored in books.

*. . . education works by a process of* **problem-solving.** Its starting point is a place where something is wrong or unsatisfactory. It is less impartial than liberal education and more keen on action and change.

*. . . the key value is* **democracy.** Teachers see themselves as helpers, people who encourage others and can offer resources as and when appropriate. The teacher is also a learner and the learner always has something to teach.

*What do its supporters say?*

Progressive educators –

– have proved their worth in their work both inside and outside the Church – social responsibility officers, industrial and agricultural chaplains, etc. Many of the pressure groups which have changed the face of the country have been started or strengthened and supported by Christians, including the consumer movement and the green/ecology lobby.
– encourage discernment and link this to living out one's faith.
– recognize God's activity as expressed primarily in the affairs of humankind in the cosmos. They may well be more interested in changing the world than in joining the Church or exploring personal faith. *Going Public*, a report on chaplaincies in Higher Education, notes that some 'see God's purpose as building a regime of love on earth and they recognise human responsibility for disharmony in the world so they become involved in political action. This is a vision of God generally active all the time and everywhere.'
– build an active, serving, caring community.

*The critics of progressive education say it is –*

– overactive. It can lead Christians to feel pangs of guilt and to rush into action before thinking clearly.
– devious. 'Guidance' and 'helping' are all very well but they may conceal a touch of manipulation.
– too sophisticated. Many people feel more secure when they can rely on an expert. It is the model of learning they are familiar with from school and is what they expect. Too much 'democracy' can be off-putting especially at the beginning. The clergy in particular are expected to 'know'.
– too visionary. The 'guide' can be wrong. Sometimes we are baffled by problems and sometimes we make serious mistakes.
– too narrow. It may concentrate on a specific problem and neglect wider issues or sources of wisdom to be found outside current experience.

– too naïve. Democracy is all very well but wisdom is not always to be found in what the majority of people think.

## Humanistic education

Another set of events:

- A training course for spiritual directors which integrates body, mind and spirit.
- Bereavement counsellors asked to write their own future epitaph, and then reflect on the experience.
- A weekend for couples on creative conflict when each alone draws up a list of 'triggers', marks them out of ten to rate their importance in the marriage, then reflects with their partner how things could be different.
- An open introductory evening on being a befriender/pastoral carer/counsellor. Includes a listening exercise in pairs where the chairs are placed so that each pair cannot see the other (plus time for reflection).
- A session on stewardship when everyone sits in a circle with their loose change in the palm of their hands while each person in turn goes round in silence taking none, some or all of the coins from each hand. There is a second round, this time to give away some, none or all that they have to anyone they wish, still in silence but registering what it feels like. Then discussion!

All these events are influenced by humanistic education.

'Humanistic' is a difficult word for many Christians. It seems to leave out the framework of Christian belief and yet it shares much of our language – words like 'growth', 'caring', 'relationships', 'empathy', 'trust', 'respect' – and with it some of the values Christians believe to be important.

*The humanistic educator believes that . . .*

*. . . the most serious problem is personal* **meaninglessness.** Too many people in too many places are denied the means of expressing their creativity by making choices, by naming, building and giving meaning to their world. Humanistic education tries to combat that by affirming the value of the

personal and stating that we all have much more power to be different and to change things than we think we have.

One of the foremost advocates of humanistic education, Carl Rogers, who as a young man trained for the ministry, tells a memorable story. While going round some neglected wards of a mental hospital he thought long and hard about why some people were there. He remembered a childhood scene repeated every year. In a basement, seed potatoes were kept from season to season in the dark. But they struggled desperately to reach any crack of light which might appear, so some grew misshapen, weak, pale shoots. But they did not give up! The impulse to live and fulfil their destiny as a potato was very strong.

*... the role of the educator is* **support.** People need to be understood and appreciated – then they will flourish. The leader's job creates the climate where natural tendencies will come to fruition. The task is to be a facilitator and enabler, a listener who, by listening, makes you more lucid. Instruction, teaching, educating, guidance are all too intrusive and presumptuous.

*... what really counts as knowledge is* **wholeness.** A word very familiar to Christians, this is variously described as personal integration, enrichment and liberation or the state of being fully-functioning, when each person becomes the very best she is capable of. St Irenaeus puts this in a Christian context: 'The glory of God is a human being fully alive, and the end of being human is the glory of God.'

*... education works by a process of* **growth.** Humanistic education is based on the belief that people are basically good (Heidegger, Buber, Sartre, Rogers and Maslow) and given enough tender loving care they will fulfil the potential they were born with. They are at the centre of the learning process. Their own experience is both the source of knowledge and the content. They want to discover, master, create and move towards self-discipline. They learn through group interaction, participation, discovery and experiment.

*... the key value is* **acceptance.** People shrivel up, become frozen and lifeless in the sharp frosts of judgement and

criticism. Nor do they want to be measured and evaluated against the standard of someone else, a teacher or a peer. The personal relationship between facilitator and learner is the key. The learner is 'prized' as are her opinions in a climate of non-possessive caring. Her feelings and struggles are articulated. Even daydreams, scolded out of us by teachers for lack of attention, are treated as 'thought's Sabbath' with something important to say.

*. . . the educated person is* **integrated.** As learners reflect on their own experience they take possession of it in a new way and gain knowledge which is authentic because it is true to life. They accept responsibility for themselves and refuse to blame other people or circumstances. 'Everyone who is 50 has responsibility for what their face looks like.' The educated person is also playful: 'Not taking yourself seriously is the only serious way to deal with life' (Hesketh Pearson).

*What do the supporters of* **humanistic** *education say?*

Humanistic educators –

–   at their best bring insights which transform people's lives. In a new Open University textbook, *Culture and Processes of Adult Learning*, Carl Rogers wrote:

> When I have been able to transform a group – and here I mean all the members of a group, myself included – into a community of learners, then the excitement has been almost beyond belief. To free curiosity; to permit learners to go charging off in new directions, dictated by their own interests; to unleash the sense of inquiry; to open everything to questioning and exploration; to recognise that everything is in process of change – here is an experience I can never forget.

–   remind us that we are one body. In theological terms group work has been described in this way: 'It illuminates God's dealings with his creatures, both men and women, and their dealings with each other; it casts fresh light on involvement and detachment, on "immanence" and "transcendence" and on "incarnation".'
–   emphasize the here and now in a way which is deeply incarnational: what is manifest is no longer downgraded. We say 'yes' to all before us in all its contingency.
–   can   combine   the   message   of   redemption   with

humanistic education so as to rescue people from limitations of mind and body in order to restore self-worth, dignity, creativity and power.
- stand against narrow economic utilitarianism, against mechanical approaches, behaviourism and determinism.
- understand that there are unconscious processes at work and seek to work with them.

*The critics of* **humanistic** *education say it –*

- is too naïve about human nature. It assumes that the devices and desires of our hearts are all benign. They are not. It ignores the divine act of redemption and healing. What is more, it assumes that knowledge is power so that if we uncover and find words to describe our experience, we will automatically release the energy and will to change our actions.
- is too naïve about the world. It does not take seriously enough the less-than-perfect real world in which we each have to live.
- is too self-centred. It has little time for other people's experience, recorded and actual, unless it supports the learners' experience or poses questions useful for further discovery. It therefore cuts itself off from very great riches. Needless to say, God's grace does not come into the picture. In fact paradoxically, it is justification by works – 'I can do it'.
- ignores institutional oppression. It is not critical of unjust structures, concentrating narrowly on the individual.
- is exclusive. Not everyone can use these insights in education (just as not everyone can be a brilliant lecturer). Teaching skills, scholarly knowledge, curricular planning, audio-visual aids, an abundance of books, useful though they are, cannot guarantee success.
- fails to nurture community, especially one of sinners who recognize their brokenness and disability even when they are seeking to be strong and empowered in the Spirit.

## Technological education

'It is the spirit of the age to believe that any fact, no matter how suspect, is superior to any imaginative exercise, no matter how true' (Gore Vidal).

Technological education is sweeping the board in commercial, industrial, public service and military contexts. It is used in systems analysis, human resources development, organizational development training and workplace training. Its purpose is to get learners to know relevant facts, skills, attitudes and beliefs. In the Church it is used in clergy and lay training.

Possible scenarios:

- A Saturday morning in an inner-city church set aside to help people who would like to read a lesson in church and who for various reasons – English is their second language, poor reading-at-sight skills, lack of confidence – are reluctant to do so (or do it badly).
- A session on aspects of accountancy for new church treasurers.
- Time spent learning how to serve at the altar.
- Preparation classes for people going to visit families of the newly baptized.
- Choir practice.

*Technological educators believe that . . .*

*. . . the most serious problem is the need for* **efficiency and productivity.** The learner is someone who needs certain skills and capacities in order to be able to adapt to a new situation and do well. Unlike some of the other models, what is going on inside the person is not the main issue. The roots of technological education are in behavioural psychology and systems theory. The goal is to be able to perform a task successfully.

*. . . the role of the educator is* **instruction.** Of all the models described, in this one the institution and the teacher have most power. Often they decide what is to be learned and how. The role of the learner is to absorb what is being taught or to copy someone who shows how the task should

be done. The task is often split up into parts to make it more manageable.

*... what really counts as knowledge is* **performance.** The test of whether or not something has been learned is the ability of the student to recall information or subscribe to the beliefs and attitudes transmitted or practise the task taught.

*... education works by a process of* **moulding.** What is to be learned is not very negotiable as it is determined by the task to be accomplished. Objectives are (or should be) clear in the mind of both teacher and student and usually described in terms of what the person will be able to do. Feedback is given from time to time as the learning progresses.

*... the key value is* **efficiency.** Unlike some other models, there is a clear basis for measuring success.

*... the educated person is* **competent.** Fuzzy amateurs are replaced by people who know what they intend to do and how to do it.

*The supporters of* **technological** *education say:*

Technological educators –
– are often, but not necessarily, those with a clear vision of the exact outcome they wish to achieve. They can with confidence proclaim an end result and then help people to respond appropriately.
– remind us that excellence has not been sufficiently valued and it should replace amateurism, overlap and wastage.
– have a vision of how it is good stewardship for Christians to develop their gifts to the utmost.
– are not frightened by accountability and scrutiny because they know where they are going and whether they get there.
– believe that the confidence gained by taking up a new role may lead to more and deeper learning later.

*The critics of **technological** education say:*

- it is not applicable to most areas of learning, since there are no clear objectives. It can distort reality by over-simplifying complex areas.
- it has no cutting edge. It does not encourage question-ing, reflection and challenge which for some people are at the heart of education.
- it is superficial. Learning answers by rote in a catechism may be skin deep.
- it is oppressive. Because the teacher chooses the 'know-ledge' and objectives, the teacher has a great deal of power against which there may be few checks and balances. Where is the place of diversity if there is one correct way? What has charisma to do with competence?
- it is too narrow. The focus is on the teacher/learner, not the wider society. This kind of education is a power-ful means of social control.

## Radical education

Once again we find Christian roots. Paulo Freire, a radical lawyer/educator, was pressured into leaving his country because of his literacy work among the poor of Brazil. His great success in teaching people to read changed the elec-toral base and had political outcomes.

Ivan Illich called for schools with their oppressive systems to be replaced by resource centres, skill exchanges, peer matching and independent educators.

Freire sees education as a way of deepening people's awareness of the sociological reality in which they live and of their capacity to change it. All educational practice has not only a theoretical stance but a political one too through 'different forms of innocence'. All education is part of social transformation, it is never neutral.

The strength of the technological tradition just described above is its taken-for-granted assumptions that 'this is the way things are done'. There is no need to talk about it. But a radical stance is different. Action/reflection is the key. It uses radical language. It castigates traditionalists as prefer-ring the dead to the living, imposed myths rather than incarnated values, the static to the dynamic, the future as a repetition of the past rather than a creative venture, gregariousness rather than authentic living together, directives rather than creative language, slogans rather than challenges.

**Radical** *educators believe that . . .*

*. . . the most serious problem is* **oppression.** Nothing less than personal and societal liberation will do. They go hand in hand.

*. . . the role of the educator is* **conscientization,** releasing the individual from a false consciousness which is unaware of the stranglehold of structural and historical forces. This is done by the teacher as facilitator and questioner rather than one who gives answers and directions. The key is mutual respect and recognition of the others' experience, knowledge and skill. All are both teachers and learners.

*. . . what really counts as knowledge is* **reflective thought and action (praxis).** It is through dialogue and engagement with society that insight into false consciousness is gained. Both teacher and learner are involved in a common search for truth and a high degree of commitment to community action. The ability to work together effectively is one desired outcome in its own right.

*. . . education works by a process of* **empowerment.** The learner's life experience is at the centre. It is questioned, re-interpreted, understood afresh in a context and acted upon. At the start group members introduce themselves and one might share the story of a relevant life experience. Other members might share their responses, examine critical issues, gather and share more information. Over a period of time the analysis deepens, the group decides together what action to take and this is followed up in group sessions. The process is used to develop a close sense of relationship between learners, encouraging self-confidence and self-worth.

Unlike progressive education, which is typically problem-solving, radical education is problem-posing. Progressive education sees that something is wrong and needs changing; radical education tries to get people to the point of seeing that something is wrong.

*. . . the key value is* **freedom.** The purpose is to enable people to act with knowledge and conviction from a viewing point which shows that there are real choices in life.

*The supporters of* **radical** *education say:*

Radical educators –
– have helped education in the way that the Green party has helped politics. Neither has been adopted on a large scale yet the influence of each is pervasive. It is no longer possible to be in education without being aware that it is never neutral and is not about keeping people happy but unchanged. It is the most powerful and truly Christian model of all because at the centre is conversion.
– point to the fact that the model of experience/reflection/action is widely accepted as an excellent tool in social and personal education, for example in secular Further Education.
– believe that because we have a heavy investment in our current status and self-image we need biblical insights combined with the strength and energy which comes from working with a group of other Christians in order to achieve a change of heart.

*The critics of* **radical** *education say:*

– it can be too narrowly political, setting up unnecessary polarization and conflict.
– it produces too much dependency. 'Co-ordinators' can become the experts upon which everyone relies and so the danger of dependency is as great as ever.
– it may lead to neglect of individual needs through its group commitment. There is not time to support anyone in a learning task which is not part of the common cause.
– it is too monolithic. Group solidarity does imply that there is a common cause and it is sceptical of pluralism.
– it has too much faith in people's inherent ability to

overcome oppression. What does freedom mean anyway
and how can it co-exist with the tradition of Christian
obedience?
- it hides the need to recognize the oppressor in ourselves. Do we distort the Story? How can we discern
  between real and imagined oppression?

## Dogmatic education

Some more events:
- A catechism being taught by rote.
- A speaker at an anti-(or pro-)abortion rally who will
  admit no interruptions or questions.
- A Bible study class where the leader reads a passage,
  tells the others what research and scholarship have to
  say, explains what the passage means and how to apply
  it to daily life. The only questions are for clarification,
  e.g., 'What did Paul mean when he said . . .?'

*The **dogmatic** educator believes that . . .*

*. . . the most serious problem is* **sin and disobedience.** There
is little human beings can do to reason out God's loving
intentions for them. Our role is to respond to a revelation
which comes from outside our limited human world and
to do that as rapidly and as fully as possible.

*. . . the role of the educator is* **proclamation.** The dogmatic
educator sees God as working through particular people or
events. The task is to underline the significance of Jesus
the Christ, the title documents of Christian tradition, credal
formulae and the historical organizational continuity of the
Church.

*. . . what really counts as knowledge is* **truth disclosed to us
through revelation.** There is a stringent responsibility to
pass on only what is truly in accordance with God's will and
to expose error.

*. . . education works by a process of* **obedience and trust.**

*. . . the key value is* **faithfulness.**

*What do its supporters say?*

Dogmatic education –
- creates strong and supportive communities by leading learners through a shared learning experience.
- provides security and certainty for those who come to faith, by giving them a basic set of tools for discipleship (like learning multiplication tables) and giving them a vision of God as friend and counsellor.
- deals creatively with a deep sense of anxiety and frustration when a nation is at odds with itself.
- integrates learning and worship, often previewing what is going to be learnt and reinforcing what has been learnt by means of a time of prayer.
- integrates personal experience, especially the leader's, with tradition.
- is faithful to revelation and tradition.

*The critics of **dogmatic** education say it –*

- is disrespectful of the God-given gifts of each person. It over-emphasizes the gulf between those who know and those who do not.
- encourages an unhealthy dependence and reliance on hierarchies but discourages a healthy questioning, thoughtful approach.
- can lead to authoritarianism, dogmatism and an abuse of power by the teacher.
- can be very hard on those who don't respond to the teaching. It may be part of a closed system of knowledge which is felt by some to fail at times, leaving disillusion and despair.

### C. A quiz

Use this quiz as an aid to going back over some key points rather than a memory test. It is the flavour of each model which needs to be recognized, not the particular wording.

1. Match each word in the left-hand column with the related word on the right:

| Type of person | Model of education |
| --- | --- |
| 'faithful' | dogmatic |
| 'responsible' | technological |
| 'competent' | liberal |
| 'integrated' | humanistic |
| 'knowledgeable' | radical |
| 'liberated' | progressive |

2.   Three of the models described see the ability to *reflect* on *experience* as a key process. Which are they?

   liberal?
   progressive?
   humanistic?
   technological?
   radical?
   dogmatic?

(See end of chapter for answer.)

3.   Each model emphasizes a different *problem.*
Which of these statements matches what has been said earlier in the chapter? (If any!)

   Liberal education primarily tackles sin and
      disobedience.

   Progressive education tackles oppression.

   Humanistic education tackles social change.

   Technological education tackles personal
      meaninglessness.

   Radical education tackles ignorance.

   Dogmatic education tackles inefficiency.

4.   Each model uses a different *process.*
Do these statements match what was said earlier?

   Liberal education is about problem-solving.

   Progressive education is about initiation.

   Humanistic education is about obedience and trust.

   Technological education is about growth.

Radical education is about moulding.

Dogmatic education is about modernization.

5. Match each key value to the appropriate tradition:

| | |
|---|---|
| liberal | efficiency |
| progressive | freedom |
| humanistic | reason |
| technological | faithfulness |
| radical | acceptance |
| dogmatic | democracy |

6. What is the educator's task in each way of working?

| | |
|---|---|
| liberal | instruction |
| progressive | transmission |
| humanistic | conscientization |
| technological | proclamation |
| radical | support |
| dogmatic | guiding |

**Chapter review**

Which of the six models has played the most important part in your life? Was it a brief intervention or did it take place over years? What can you learn from that experience? Which of the six models do you feel most committed to now? And which the least?

Which is the most appropriate way ahead for the people you have some responsibility for now? Are there gaps which you cannot fill? Can you co-operate with others who can help? What has to be left to 'sanctified neglect'?

The chapters that follow are designed to help you to work out what it means to practise one or more of these strands in real-life situations.

(Answer to question 2: progressive, humanistic and radical.)

# 3

# How Adults Learn

This chapter has two sections:

A. *Ten factors which help adults to learn*
B. *Widely held beliefs about the way adults learn*

'Have you, over the last few months, spent at least seven hours trying to learn, understand or get the hang of something new to the point where you could teach another person a bit about it?'

This simple question was the basis of some interesting Canadian research into informal learning. At first many people said they hadn't done any. But given a little time to think about it, and with a modest degree of prompting, many began to realize they had. They had not all attended courses, and some had learned in spite of the training or education they had received. Turning up at an event does not necessarily mean a commitment to learning and change. Too often it is as if we present a road map to a person who has no intention of making the journey but is too polite to say so.

## A. *Ten factors which help adults to learn, using the mnemonic* REVELATION.

### 1. R is for *relevance*

*People learn best when they can see the point of what they are doing*: in other words, they are learning in ways that are *relevant* for them.

Adults usually learn in order to cope better with real-life situations or to get answers to questions which will not go away. Gone are the days when they had to attend classes or when they were working for some distant goal.

Even so, what gets people interested in learning is more complicated. We are not always rational beings, making the most time- and cost-effective choice. Our motives are usually very mixed.

Christians may join a group or class out of loyalty to the vicar even though it is on an inconvenient night and the subject is not high on a list of priorities. Or they may go because as Christians they feel they ought to ask the questions being raised. They may go out of curiosity or to see a friend or because it is a convenient place to be while waiting to give someone a lift.

It is so easy to be blinded by churchy concerns when drawing up a programme. Christians need to be constantly listening out for current concerns, in the life of the nation, the neighbourhood and the individual person. Not just because it is good adult education practice (which it is) and because people will be more likely to respond (which they will) but because that is where the gospel is to be lived out day by day. Where else?

## 2. E is for *experience*

*People learn best when experience is used to illuminate and earth practice.* It does it in a way nothing else can.

In adult education there is, as someone put it nicely, a form of 'existential drift', a vague but nevertheless powerful pull towards life. 'Learning is the process whereby knowledge is created through the transformation of experience' is David Kolb's useful definition.

There is research evidence that people attach more meaning to learnings linked to experience than those acquired passively. But that may slow up the process. Adults' rich experience of life means that as new knowledge comes their way, time is needed to check it out against what they already know. A talk on Church history may present new and disturbing patterns of looking at familiar local buildings. Was this building, now a theological college, really built on the profits of the slave trade? Does this Christian conference centre stand because it was originally built from profits gained from exploiting miners and their families? A speaker's Christology may be 'higher' or 'lower' than that of the hearers. Or a lecture on faith development may conflict with what they know about young people or old age.

But this web of connectedness is what makes learning stick. It drives the engine which provides the energy to move, to toss ideas about, to walk around a familiar landscape and see it afresh from another perspective. In other words, the uncritical acceptance of what someone else says (or said in the past) is replaced by the adult's own meanings and conclusions. A living faith earthed in daily life replaces a stock of second-hand, if precious, concepts.

## 3. V is for *variety*

*Adults learn best when they are offered a variety of opportunities.*

The learner's current situation influences what is possible. Adults may participate intermittently because of domestic or work commitments. They may not have benefited much from their initial education and need help to get started. Practical help may include: transport, convenient times and places, help with finance and home care, flexible ways of study (including open and distance learning) and a range of teaching methods.

## 4. E is for *enjoyment*

*People learn best when they are in a reasonably comfortable welcoming atmosphere.*

We may well have a stock of memories of outstanding speakers listened to while standing in the rain or sessions when the content was so good we forgot the uncomfortable chairs or the cigarette smoke or the cold.

But as a rule we need to pay attention to:

- warmth;
- colour and light;

- rhythm and pattern: time to talk, be silent, enjoy music, etc.;
- balance: large meetings, small, time alone, large again, etc.;
- order: things which begin and end when they say they will, clear 'contracts' so that things happen as promised;
- unity: a central theme which knits sections together, a clear path linking and carrying things forward;
- a sense of welcome.

One message of the incarnation is that this worldly creation should not be downgraded and that we can say 'yes' to what is before us. There is an ancient Jewish saying that when we reach heaven we shall be required to give reasons for all the good and pleasurable things God had prepared for us which we refused and rejected.

### 5. L is for *learning skills*

*People learn best when they are given help with learning skills, which they probably were not taught at school.*

Most of us have never been taught how to learn; we do not know that we have unrealized potential. Here are a few pointers:

### Reading

Some books need to be read from beginning to end but not all. Lord Balfour said 'He has only half learned the art of reading who has not added to it the even more refined accomplishments of skipping and skimming'. Nor are illustrated books necessarily lightweight.

### Essay-writing

It has its own conventions. What does the last word of this instruction mean: 'The only reason why there was not an English Revolution like the French Revolution was the rise of Methodism. Discuss'? For at least one student, who knew a lot about the subject, a discussion meant a conversation between two or more people. Yet all there was was a blank sheet of paper. Not much of a sparring partner . . .

## Making notes

Some people set out ideas in clear note form, with headings and sub-headings. But others have been helped by Tony Buzan's 'brain patterns', and encouraged to write the main theme of a sermon or subject in the centre of the page. After that any thoughts worth exploring are noted down on lines like branches of a tree. Students can make their own connections.

## Clutter

Clutter was once described as 'the greatest blight on human thinking'. Help may be needed in sorting out the wood from the trees. Tasks may need to be broken down into smaller pieces: read through what you have written, for example, three times, once asking is it true? then, is it relevant? and, lastly, can it be understood? Do not try to do all three at once.

## 6. A is for *acceptance*

*People learn best when they feel themselves to be accepted for what they are.* Then they feel secure and can try out things in safety.

Adults enter a learning situation with many roles, as workers, citizens, parents, neighbours, priests. They are used to being required to know about things. They see themselves as responsible, dependable adults and this is challenged when they become learners. The situation is made worse if they were patronized or humiliated when they were at school

What is needed is 'a place of safety'. There is an art in arranging things so that the learner is willing to bring to the surface thoughts and feelings which lie buried, covered with fears about adequacy. ('What will they think if I say "I don't understand"?') On the other hand security has to be balanced by challenge. There has to be a manageable degree of uncertainty: the benefits of exploring new and better ways must outweigh the risks involved. Adults need to be reassured that mistakes are worth making for the sake of learning. The good tutor enables the group to support and challenge each other.

## 7. T is for *tutoring skills*

*Adults learn best when tutors practise what they preach.*

The lecturer who takes an hour and 50 minutes to say that the best attention span for adults is 20 minutes really does exist!

Tutors are not expected to know everything and are respected for saying they cannot answer a question. While good planning, preparation and communication should not be optional extras, beware of doing too much for students: perfect planning, endless handouts, always making the running, unfailing charisma.

Enthusiasm for the subject and a willingness to learn from others as well as to teach also helps. There is one other skill, however, which is very important: the understanding that learning spills out all over the place and is not confined to the subject matter or the learning slot. It is often called the hidden curriculum.

We ask ourselves 'What shall I teach?' and make careful choices. We also need to be continually asking: 'What are people learning from the way that I teach and indeed from the person I am?' Of course it is not all in our control.

Suppose someone has just finished a well-prepared talk on St Paul's missionary journeys. Six different students might say:

– I learned that it is useful to look for several causes of an event rather than stop when I have found one.
– I learned to be a bit more careful in my use of words. New Testament Greek would be very useful. I wonder if I should ask if I can have some lessons?
– I learned that this subject is too difficult for me. She goes too fast. I might have to drop out.
– I learned not to make sweeping generalizations. Some of the things I've always believed are plain wrong. The Church for me has always meant what goes on here. I begin to see in a new way how we are part of something bigger.

- I learned that it is all right to make a mistake in this group. I took a risk when I asked that question. Mistakes are useful because they show up where I need to turn my attention. Now I do understand about Paul's intentions. I shall ask questions again.
- I learned that there are some interesting people here whom I would like to know better. Even so I am not sure I know what they are on about.

Which of these six people have learned what the speaker intended? Probably the first, fourth and fifth, though they could all have been learnt from the same person talking on a wide range of subjects, nothing to do with St Paul. The third response is certainly unintended and the sixth is likely to be. Lastly, the speaker may have had it in mind to tempt people into learning Greek (the second response) or the request may come as a surprise.

None of us is perfectly consistent or totally aware of what is going on in a learning situation. But people learn best when we try to be aware of the total effect of what we are doing.

### 8. I is for *individual differences*

*People learn best when individual progress is affirmed.*

If possible arrange the course in a series of relatively easy steps and with built-in goals for success at the beginning. Evaluation helps identify what has been done so far and may mark out what the next steps might be. It describes and does not judge. If learning events are shaped so that they are useful and rewarding as soon as possible, the learner is likely to persevere.

For example, time may be a problem. There may be more or less of it from week to week, according to work or family or health considerations. Nothing is easier than to build up guilt unless allowance is made for differences. The tasks set must be manageable and comparisons with other students discouraged. Some may have to cope with the pain of 'unlearning', i.e., questioning and dismantling ideas and values which are part of an inner core of taken-for-granted assumptions. Someone needs to fine-tune the programme to meet individual needs and capabilities, to counsel and encourage.

## 9. O is for *opportunities*

*People learn best when there are opportunities for practising and so reinforcing what has been learned.*

This is easier in on-the-job training but small-group discussion can be included, where people are given time to try out information and ideas they have just learned from someone in authority: what does it mean for a Christian to be a warden or to work in the World Bank; to be a curate or the conductor of the 109 bus from Croydon to Trafalgar Square?

Learning can sometimes result in frustration if it is unrecognized. New patterns of ministry and leadership are talked about but they may bear little relation to what happens back home in the local church. Sometimes people are only accepted on courses if they are sponsored by their local leaders or congregations. Past experience has shown that there are too many dashed hopes and disillusioned people otherwise.

If adult education is modular, in short bursts of an hour, a day, a weekend, a few weeks, or part-time over a period of months and so interleaved with everything else going on, it is more likely to be worked out in practice.

## 10. N is for *nurture*

*People learn best when they are given the chance to nurture and teach others.*

Passing on what has been learned may happen informally in the home or the workplace or the church. It may be done by being a member of a congregational group welcoming newcomers to the faith, as in the Catechumenate movement, or by helping a tutor with her research/learning. And some will have specific responsibility because of their role in the nurture and teaching of the Body of Christ.

So we come back to the mnemonic . . .

**R** elevance
**E** xperience
**V** ariety
**E** njoyment
**L** earning skills
**A** cceptance
**T** utoring skills
**I** ndividual differences
**O** pportunities to act
**N** urture others

## B. *Things people say*

'You can't teach an old dog new tricks.'

'I have a memory like a sieve, always have and always will.'

'Although I am chairman of the Education Committee, every time I visit a headteacher and walk through their study door, I feel like a little boy again.'

'Adults judge the value of learning by whether they can use it or not.'

'The best way to understand something is to memorize it.'

'I notice that several of us in this new group have been through more than our fair share of upheaval in the past few months.'

### Is it true?

*'You can't teach an old dog new tricks.'*

Yes you can. There is now a fairly good consensus that most adults can learn what they would have learnt as young people, with some exceptions: fast, complex skills, and skills dependent on physical attributes which deteriorate with age, such as perfect eyesight. In addition older people may be less good at memorizing, less used to concentrating and less adaptable.

The good news is that they may be more sure of what they want, have more time, be better organized, better able to make effective decisions and socially more skilled. The more these increments can be made use of the better.

A mass of research evidence shows that what happens to our learning abilities depends on several factors including:

– self-confidence,
– access to appropriate teaching methods,
– physiological changes (some of which can be compensated for),
– lack of external sanctions (which means more reliance on inner motivation).

*'I have a memory like a sieve, always have and always will.'*

The 'always will' can be changed. What is experienced by each of us – pictures, thoughts, sounds, feelings – is retained in our 'memory' ready for future use. Remembering is finding them when we want them.

The cause of a learner's poor memory may be:

(a)  The item never went into store properly in the first place, because either it was not properly understood, or it was of no interest or importance. We know that the brain organizes its knowledge of the world in categories, almost as if it operates an internal filing system. It is as if the file never got there in the first place. Shakespeare called memory 'the warder of the brain'.

(b)  Memories can be overlaid with more recent learning which interferes with what we have already laid down.

(c)  We may also forget because we have a lot of similar information to sift through. Then we must be strict about stripping down to essentials and clearing away clutter.

(d)  A particularly hard case is when new material conflicts with what is already known. Then existing opinions can 'interfere' with learning, making it more difficult to come to terms with new ideas.

(e)  There are 'simple' explanations too like tiredness, illness, anxiety about failure, lack of confidence, poor history of past success, etc.

(f)  A lot of learning material is not set out in helpful ways. Mnemonics like 'REVELATION' may not be very profound but they can be pegs to hang ideas on so they don't get lost.

*'Although I am chairman of the Education Committee, every time I visit a headteacher and walk through their study door, I feel like a little boy again.'*

This remark is one rather dramatic example of the many ways in which people recall childhood experiences when the words 'education' or 'learning' are mentioned. All of us failed some of the time and some of us failed all of the time. People in authority are often seen as blamers and punishers.

This works both to stop people coming to events in the first place and also to narrow their idea of what might happen when they do turn up. They may expect to sit in rows and be told what to do and how to think. They may not realize they have all sorts of gifts and graces which were unrecognized or not present in childhood.

*'Adults judge the value of learning by whether they can use it or not.'*

This is largely true if you accept a broad definition of the word 'use'. Going to a Bible study class may be 'useful' if you want to learn more about the Bible or impress your fiancée or get to know your neighbours better or find out whether or not you would like to train as an elder or reader or preacher or evangelist or pastoral worker. Our motives are often mixed.

But there is another serious point behind all this. Do people want learning to be useful in the sense that they can change it into a sort of currency and cash it in in order to be able to take up a new role in the church, such as pastoral visitor or ordained minister? Some people undoubtedly do, and others are pleased to find, for example, that a Bishop's Certificate Course counts as an A level when applying for access to a college of Higher Education.

*'The best way to understand something is to memorize it.'*

This really should be turned on its head: 'The best way to memorize something is to understand it.' Understanding is to do with learning how to handle ideas, make connections and see patterns. But memory provides the items to toss around: prayers, passages of scriptures, writings, pictures and diagrams. They are the tapes we have with us every-where on our internal Sony Walkman. They are easier to acquire the younger you are but perfectly possible at any age.

*'I notice that several of us in this new group have been through more than our fair share of upheaval in the last few months.'*

Any change – either gradual like growing older or sudden like an accident; sad like a bereavement or happy like the birth of a child – may challenge people to come to terms with life in a new way. They may need to move away from the rules and expectations which had served them well enough in the past in order to become 'owners of their true selves'. The older we get the more life experiences we have in common – friendship, marrying, parenting, loss – and yet the more distinctive our own pattern becomes. At any point along the path we may become disorientated or dissatisfied, gradually or suddenly.

One researcher speaks of transformation happening through a series of steps:

- Something happens, good or bad, suddenly or over time, which unsettles and disorientates us. We may have chosen it or it may have been forced upon us.
- We reflect on what has happened.
- We begin to look critically at our taken-for-granted assumptions about ourselves and about what is expected of us by others.
- We relate what is happening to similar experiences of others and to what is going on in public life, recognizing that one's situation is shared by others and is never a purely private matter.
- We explore optional new ways of being and doing.
- We begin to build experience and confidence in new ways of being.
- We plan a course of action.
- We get the skills and knowledge to implement the plan.
- We try out the new roles and get people's reaction.
- We reintegrate into society on a new basis dictated by a new purpose.

This research was based on women who re-entered work. Some of the women had suffered the death of a husband or divorce or the incapacitation of a breadwinner. For others there was a more evolutionary history of gradually coming to terms with what was expected of them as things changed in society, combined with the melting of inner assumptions about what was right and proper. The ten-step process just as accurately describes other circumstances where there is a major life change, such as the call to ordination.

This chapter began and ended with a brief reference to research projects. The next chapter moves from the general to the particular, moving away from what we have in common as learners to the ways in which people use different strategies.

# 4

# Learning Styles

This chapter has four parts:

A. *A four-stage learning or pastoral cycle*
   The place of experience, reflection, review and action in adult religious education.
B. *Learning styles questionnaire*
   A way of discovering your own preferred style of learning through the Honey and Mumford questionnaire, and of appreciating its implications for your work as a tutor/facilitator.
C. *The link between style and method*
   The relationship between the way people learn and the type of event which would be most helpful for them.
D. *Learning opportunities*
   The importance of providing a range of learning opportunities.

## A. *A four-stage learning cycle*

In recent years our understanding of how adults learn has undergone a revolution. A formative text was 'Towards an applied theory of experiential learning' by David Kolb and Ronald Frey of the Massachusetts Institute of Technology, who identified a four-part process:

   experiencing,
   reflecting,
   theorizing and
   action.

The experiential learning model they devised has been widely accepted as a practical tool. Its importance is in its emphasis on the fact that 'learning and change result from the integration of emotional experiences with cognitive processes: conceptual analysis and understanding'.

Two British educationalists, Peter Honey and Alan Mumford, took the learning-cycle theory further in their publications, but above all in workshops and consultations in many different contexts in the past decade. Below, each of the four stages is described. It may look as though they are in order, following one after the other. That is misleading. In practice learners can start anywhere and switch between them rapidly. There is an endless cycle of events since each experience changes us and we start afresh with new insights.

Honey and Mumford also point out another interesting fact. Not only do we have a preferred learning style (or styles) but that is the one we are most comfortable with when teaching others. We think of our own experience as typical and so imagine we are being most helpful when we draw on it. In fact what helped us may not be the best or only way for others.

## 1. Experiencing

Whatever we do we filter new information through our memory banks of previous experiences. Reading this book is a handy example: what makes sense will be retained and threaded into our theories, changing our practice. Anything else will be rejected and forgotten since it strikes us as either irrelevant or inaccurate.

## 2. Reflecting

But experience alone is not enough – as the proverbs say, it may make a wise person wiser but it also confirms fools in their foolishness. It may require deep personal stock-taking. The 20-year-old student weeps in his tutor's room because his divorcing parents have torn up his childhood history of a happy family life, precious holidays and Christmases, now saying it was all a sham. A few years later he and they may recognize that some truth lies in both stories: there was a great deal of happiness *and* it was far from perfect. We ponder our experience to make sense of a messy and complicated process, sometimes alone, sometimes one to one and sometimes in a safe group.

## 3. Reviewing

This is the time for drawing things together into a framework which makes sense, perhaps considering several options, choosing one and being able to justify the choice. This is where theories and models come into their own as we hold each one up as a lens through which to view what is before us. At this stage we draw conclusions from the experience.

## 4. Taking action

All of us, learners and tutors alike, are changed in some way by the learning process. We may as a result make a conscious decision to do or be something different. It may be that we are testing out our conclusions to see if they work. If they don't we can drop them, if they do they become part of us. Either way our experience is always new and the cycle continues.

*Some are pragmatists* . . . Miners' wives in the North East and the East Midlands at the time of the miners' strike in the 1980s wanted to change what was going on around them. Together they provided food and clothing for their children, and the experience led them to reflect on wider issues and plan increasingly effective action in the future.

*Some are reflectors* . . . Women who read the *Guardian* in the 1960s exchanged ideas and then started pressure groups, civic amenity watchdogs and local and national campaigns. Other gingered up political parties.

*Some are theorists* . . . people who sit in libraries and studies, argue and discuss with colleagues.

*Some are activists* . . . evangelists who learn on the job, chaplains who confront new and unexpected situations.

## B. *The questionnaire*

### How to discover your own learning style

This questionnaire was devised by Peter Honey and Alan Mumford (see Further Reading on p. 131): what is provided here is but a taster. The exercise may take about 10–20 minutes to complete. There are no right and wrong answers: the results simply offer a comparison with other people. Tick what, on balance, you agree with. If you disagree more than agree put a cross. If you cannot decide, leave a blank, but only as a last resort.

### Learning styles questionnaire

1 I often take reasonable risks, if I feel it is justified. ☐

2 I tend to solve problems using a step-by-step approach, avoiding any fanciful ideas. ☐

3 I have a reputation for having a no-nonsense direct style. ☐

4 I often find that actions based on feelings are as sound as those based on careful thought and analysis. ☐

5 The key factor in judging a proposed idea or solution is whether it works in practice or not. ☐

6 When I hear about a new idea or approach I like to start working out how to apply it in practice as soon as possible. ☐

7 I like to follow a self-disciplined approach, establish clear routines and logical thinking patterns. ☐

8 I take pride in doing a thorough, methodical job. ☐

9 I get on best with logical, analytical people, and less well with spontaneous, 'irrational' people. ☐

10 I take care over the interpretation of data available to me, and avoid jumping to conclusions. ☐

11 I like to reach a decision carefully after weighing up many alternatives. ☐

12 I'm attracted more to new, unusual ideas than to practical ones. ☐

13 I dislike situations that I cannot fit into a coherent pattern. ☐

14 I like to relate my actions to a general principle. ☐

15 In meetings I have a reputation for going straight to the point, no matter what others feel. ☐

16 I prefer to have as many sources of information as possible – the more data to consider the better. ☐

17 Flippant people who don't take things seriously enough usually irritate me. ☐

18 I prefer to respond to events on a spontaneous, flexible basis rather than plan things out in advance. ☐

19 I dislike very much having to present my conclusions under the time pressure of tight deadlines, when I could have spent more time thinking about the problem. ☐

20 I usually judge other people's ideas principally on their practical merits. ☐

21 I often get irritated by people who want to rush headlong into things. ☐

22 The present is much more important than thinking about the past or future. ☐

23 I think that decisions based on a thorough analysis of all the information are sounder than those based on intuition. ☐

24 In meetings I enjoy contributing ideas to the group, just as they occur to me. ☐

25 On balance I tend to talk more than I should, and ought to develop my listening skills. ☐

26 In meetings I get very impatient with people who lose sight of the objectives. ☐

27 I enjoy communicating my ideas and opinions to others. ☐

28 People in meetings should be realistic, keep to the point, and avoid indulging in fancy ideas and speculations. ☐

29 I like to ponder many alternatives before making up my mind. ☐

30 Considering the way my colleagues react in meetings, I reckon on the whole I am more objective and unemotional. ☐

31 At meetings I'm more likely to keep in the background than to take the lead and do most of the talking. ☐

32 On balance I prefer to do the listening rather than the talking. ☐

33 Most times I believe the end justifies the means. ☐

34 Reaching the group's objectives and targets should take precedence over individual feelings and objections. ☐

35 I do whatever seems necessary to get the job done. ☐

36 I quickly get bored with methodical, detailed work. ☐

37 I am keen on exploring the basic assumptions, principles and theories underpinning things and events. ☐

38 I like meetings to be run on methodical lines, sticking to laid-down agendas. ☐

39 I steer clear of subjective or ambiguous topics. ☐

40 I enjoy the drama and excitement of a crisis. ☐

This questionnaire is an adaptation of the Learning Styles Questionnaire published in *The Manual of Learning Styles*, by P. Honey and A. Mumford (1992; available from Dr P. Honey, Ardingley House, 10 Linden Avenue, Maidenhead, Berkshire SL6 6HB).

Now see how you score. Score one point for each item you ticked. There are no points for items you crossed or left blank. Add up each column and double the total. You should have four figures, one under each of the headings. Turn to the section on which you scored highest for a description of that type of learner.

*Score Chart*

| 1 | | 8 | | 2 | | 3 | |
|---|---|---|---|---|---|---|---|
| 4 | | 10 | | 7 | | 5 | |
| 12 | | 11 | | 9 | | 6 | |
| 18 | | 16 | | 13 | | 15 | |
| 22 | | 19 | | 14 | | 20 | |
| 24 | | 21 | | 17 | | 26 | |
| 25 | | 23 | | 30 | | 28 | |
| 27 | | 29 | | 37 | | 33 | |
| 36 | | 31 | | 38 | | 34 | |
| 40 | | 32 | | 39 | | 35 | |
| Total Activist | | Total Reflector | | Total Theorist | | Total Pragmatist | |

*Final Score Chart*

| Activist | Reflector | Theorist | Pragmatist | |
|---|---|---|---|---|
| 20 | 20 | 20 | 20 | |
| 18 | | | | |
| 16 | | 18 | | very strong preference |
| | | | 18 | |
| 14 | | | | |
| | 18 | 16 | | |
| 12 | | | 16 | |
| | 16 | | | strong preference |
| | | 14 | | |

*Continued overleaf*

*Final Score Chart Continued*

| Activist | Reflector | Theorist | Pragmatist | |
|---|---|---|---|---|
| 10 | 14 | | 14 | |
| | | 12 | | moderate preference |
| 8 | | | | |
| | 12 | | 12 | |
| 6 | | 10 | | |
| | 10 | | 10 | low preference |
| 4 | | 8 | | |
| | 8 | | 8 | |
| | | 6 | | |
| | 6 | | 6 | |
| 2 | | 4 | | very low preference |
| | 4 | | 4 | |
| | 2 | 2 | 2 | |
| 0 | 0 | 0 | 0 | |

## C. *The link between learning styles and methods*

*Activists learn best when . . .*

. . . there is *challenge*. Their motto is 'I'll try anything once'. They enjoy being thrown in at the deep end with an idea or a problem they have not met before. They like *variety* so that they can switch from one activity to another before they get too bored. They feel confident about being *in the limelight* so they are happy to be asked to chair a discussion or give a talk. They also enjoy being *part of a team*, bouncing ideas around with other people. They are better at coming up with ideas if they are allowed for the time being to forget whether it is practical or not: the shortage of money, the fact that 'people will not like it', the routine work necessary to carry it out. They are *enthusiastic* and *open-minded*.

*Activists learn least well when . . .*

. . . they are asked to stand back and *not* be *involved*. They are not keen on listening or being shown how things should be done. They would rather have a go themselves. Nor do they like *working alone*. And whereas being given *precise instructions* and a lot of *detail* gives some people a feeling of security, activists feel swamped and cramped, with little room for manoeuvre. As they thrive on novelty, they will not appreciate being told that 'practice makes perfect', especially if it involves *routine and repetition*. And it's probably not wise to ask them to attend to all the loose ends, dotting the *i*-s and crossing the *t*-s. They prefer not to be given too much *theory* nor are they very keen on quietly *assessing* beforehand what they will learn nor on *reflecting* afterwards to consolidate what they have learned.

*Reflectors learn best when . . .*

. . . they are given *time and space* to stand back and reflect on what is going on, whether it is watching a video or a demonstration, listening to a discussion or a talk. They need to be allowed to *think* before acting, to *consider* a number of angles on a subject and to have all the information possible about it before giving an answer. Their motto is 'Look before you leap'. They like time to *prepare*, to read things beforehand, a chance to do a bit of *research* even if it means some painstaking and unexciting work. They have the energy to get to the bottom of things, to 'do things properly'. They are happy to exchange views and ask questions, etc., only if it can be done without danger, i.e., if it is done by prior agreement and they know exactly where they stand because the instructions are clear. Otherwise they keep a *low profile*. When they do join in they may well use the chance to present other people's views as well as their own. They take a *broad view* but will come to their own decision provided they are not put under pressure and given tight deadlines.

*Reflectors learn least well when . . .*

. . . they are forced into the *limelight* or asked to do things *without* any *warning*. They find it difficult when asked to give instant reactions, first impressions or what the media love, the sound bite. They become uneasy if time is short and a session is *rushed* through using short cuts or dealing with a subject just on the surface. They may dislike *variety*, being moved from one activity or speaker to another before they have had a chance to consider the matter in depth. They may feel resentful if they are asked to come to a conclusion or give an answer when they have *not* been given *enough information.*

### *Theorists learn best when . . .*

. . . they can listen to or read ideas which are well thought out and *logical.* They like being offered a theory, a *pattern of ideas* which they can follow step by step, question, explore and consider. They also enjoy being asked to make their own *connections* between ideas and situations. Checking a paper for inconsistencies would be regarded as an enjoyable task. So too would be being asked to understand a *complicated* problem. They are the sort of people who would jump at the chance to ask *searching questions* about what was being taught, including what was being taken for granted. Nor do they mind their own ideas being questioned because they like to be intellectually *stretched.* They enjoy the freedom to play with ideas even when these are not strictly speaking to do with the matter in hand. On the other hand they will not rest easy until things are *neat and tidy*, all the details tucked into a scheme.

### *Theorists learn least well when . . .*

. . . policies, principles and ideas are *not explained,* or when they are *not given the evidence* to support an argument, for example figures or facts which can be questioned. So statements based on *feelings or intuition* may not be given much weight. *Open-minded questions* which cannot be settled by logic may also result in too many feelings of uncertainty for much learning to take place. They are uncomfortable too if they find the subject is dealt with in a *shallow* way, ignoring questions, or if *contradictory ideas or methods* are presented. They may also find themselves out of tune with other people in the group, especially activists.

*Pragmatists learn best when . . .*

. . . they are working on something which will give them ideas and skills they can try out in *practice.* Opportunities to get cracking at once are welcome. The subject must be *linked clearly with the job or the problem* they have in hand, otherwise it may not be taken seriously. And they are looking for *techniques* which will give a quick and reliable return: e.g., how to save time, how to interview, how to counsel in difficult situations. They are good at picking up *new ideas* and giving them the benefit of the doubt while they try them out in real life. They enjoy learning from a video or a person *showing how to do the job well,* particularly if that person has a proven track record of success. *Stories and examples* of how things worked out in the past are an encouragement. They are the sort of people who return to the local congregation after being on a course on stewardship or counselling, brimming with enthusiasm and dying to try out all the new ideas.

*Pragmatists learn least well when . . .*

. . . they *cannot see* how what they are asked to learn is going to be of any *practical help* to them. It may be that they *cannot see how it fits in* with their situation or, if it does, it seems not to bring any reward. They like to get on with things and get impatient with *long-winded argument, discussion going round in circles and complicated theories.* They are down to earth and may see those who teach them as out of touch, all talk and chalk. Clear guidelines are welcomed. If the session is teaching them something which clearly does work they will lose interest if they think that, for whatever reason, they are *not allowed to try things out.*

### D. *Learning opportunities*

It is important to provide a range of learning opportunities to match the needs of different people.

*Activists* tend to like:

role play
simulation games
competitive team games
drama
sculpting
buzz groups
workshops
brainstorming
projects
visits

*Reflectors* tend to like:

good briefing
discussions
debates
panels of experts
group interviews
'T' groups
film
video
computer programmes
research possibilities
libraries
one-to-one work with a tutor
distance learning
opportunities for active listening/dialogue
counselling

*Theorists* tend to like:

lectures
a guided reading list
programmed learning
tutorials
supervision
help with note-taking
sermons
seminars

***Pragmatists*** *tend to like:*

case studies
demonstrations
on-the-job training
meeting the expert
workshops
agenda-making
instruction
training seminars
incident-making
problem-solving

We are all different mixtures of the four styles which may mean that a description of one style will not wrap neatly around us. St Paul's insistence that we must be all things to all people and that in the Body of Christ there are many different gifts means that when it comes to helping people learn, we are faced with a demanding and stimulating task.

# 5

---

# Strategies for Learning

This chapter consists of a menu of 25 different ways of learning. It describes each in turn, listing advantages and weaknesses. Where appropriate, this is followed by a specific example.

Items should not be plucked off the shelf at random. Always start by questioning the purpose of the session, the amount of time you can reasonably give to preparation, the skills you and the group have (and do not have) and the limitations of the place where you are meeting. Beware too of using a method as a leader which you have not already experienced as a participant and of thinking that there is a perfect answer to every educational event, if only you had enough training, skill, experience, money and time. In the last resort there are processes at work which are beyond our control, which is a humbling and comforting thought when we are tempted to believe it all depends on us. Learners ultimately make their own choices. Our responsibility is to set out before them as many opportunities as we can.

## 1. Agenda group

People meet together to identify what it is they need to learn. If the group is large it may be useful to split into smaller groups, each focusing on an area which is of special interest to them. At the beginning they may draw up a list which is too long. Then conversations begin about what is feasible.

*Advantages*

- There is a greater commitment to the task because the learning meets a real need, not an imagined one. If people take part in making decisions, they are more likely to carry them out than if they are asked to join something dreamed up by someone else.
- The unexpected can happen. It might reveal that there are more resources (perhaps within the group) and more time than was originally foreseen.
- Or it might show up the limitations of what is possible before too many hopes have been raised.

*Disadvantages*

- It takes time which might be spent getting on with the course.
- The leader may be faced with following up such a meeting with frantic activity trying to respond to what was asked for. It may be easier just to offer a course and hope for the best.

*Example*

The first session of a course for parish visitors could be used to clarify some of the issues to be covered:

Why do people need visits in the first place? Is it for their benefit or the church's or both?

Who should do it? What is special about a visit from the clergy?

What lies behind this?

What are the particular needs of this place?

What makes a 'good' visit?

What experience do people in the room have of parish visiting and how can it help not hinder other members' learning?

What not to do!

Practical help with listening skills.

Rules about what is confidential.

How to care for someone who is asking for more time than it is possible to give.

How to cope with rebuff.

Where to go if more help is needed *and so on* . . .

An agenda group not only sorts out a list of things but gives some idea of the order in which they should be tackled, what skills there are in the group which can be used to help everyone and how time should be allocated.

## 2. Audio cassette

This may bring into the room music, plays, poetry, interviews, sermons, lectures from people past and present and from many countries. It may need pauses to allow the listener to think or express their reactions out loud before hearing what the tape goes on to say.

### Advantages

- It is useful if you are learning alone because a tape can be played on a journey, in bed, almost anywhere if you have a machine.
- It is cheap to make or to buy and can be sent easily through the post. This means that members of a group can use tapes as a basis for homework between sessions, discussing their reactions when they meet.

### Disadvantages

- If you are in a group where do you look when you are listening to a tape? We are used to hearing and not seeing but only when we are active ourselves, for example on the telephone, driving or doing the ironing.
- It is hard to concentrate for long. A person speaking to us gets the feel of our reaction and may sense when to stop to allow questions or discussion. But sometimes tapes seem to get a life of their own and leaders feel shy about interrupting them.
- Acoustics may be a problem.

## 3. Bible study – participatory

This is a way of linking the academic study of Scripture with the issues of daily life. It is based on the belief that the Bible has a far richer and more subtle authority than that of rule book and manual. Through meditation, painting, drama, role play, writing, group work, music and a host of other ways the Bible is encountered as a creative, dynamic authority, bringing new worlds into view and enabling participants to enter them. The term 'participatory Bible study' is a portmanteau phrase covering a lot of different events. There is a network of people who are workshop leaders and they meet regularly to share and improve theory and practice.

*Advantages*

- These methods can reach parts other methods do not reach. The aim is to touch the whole person, body, mind and spirit.
- People who have always believed that they cannot paint, write poetry, model with clay or enjoy drama discover new skills which can be used again and again in later years.
- It does not depend on being able to read.

*Disadvantages*

- This approach is not a bag of tricks to enliven a session but can only be used by those who have themselves done some training, have the necessary personal gifts and have thought through their actions carefully. Workshops can be very powerful events as people may express feelings and attitudes which take them by surprise.
- Premises, lighting and equipment need to be chosen with care. Transporting clay or paints or sheets of plastic around can be tiresome.
- Timing needs to be handled sensitively to ensure that everybody gets a chance to share – things can get out of hand if one or two characters take up most of the attention.

*Example*

A group reads together Matthew 20.1–16, the parable of the Workers in the Vineyard.

They are then asked to imagine themselves as one of the workers: someone who worked from the early morning or one who joined in at the sixth hour or one of those who came in right at the end but still got the same wage.

In these three groups they discuss what God's justice and provision means for them both as individuals and as part of an economic system.

The three groups then join together and conduct a silent discussion. Instead of talking they write messages to each other. One of the walls of the room is covered in sheets of blank paper. It is divided into three columns. Anyone can go up and write a comment on what they have discovered from the passage. Contributions from other people might or might not be comments on what has already been written. Gradually a powerful picture emerges as the groups struggle with their different experiences of work and reward.

What is powerful is the presence of everyone's contribution up in front. Some may be struggling with how God's grace relates to our feeling that we have to 'earn' our way into life; others may point out how economic structures invisibly work to reinforce fears of whole categories of workers who see themselves as inferior and unworthy.

Variations would be to study alongside the Bible newspaper cuttings on these issues; to encourage people to write their own prayer, poem, parable or psalm in response to what they have learned; or to express some aspect of the truth of the passage in paint, clay or drama.

## 4. Brainstorming

A small to medium-size group (8 to 20 people) is presented with a problem and asked to suggest solutions, no matter how far-fetched some of them may seem. Each idea is welcomed and recorded, perhaps on a flip chart. It is not discussed at this point, nor is anyone allowed to object or pour cold water on the idea.

Once people enter into the spirit of suggesting the first

idea that comes into their head, no matter how ridiculous they may think it is, this method can be fun. There should be no unkind laughter. If it is safe to say what they want to say, even the more timid ones will join in. Leaders themselves might like to contribute one or two unusual solutions so as to get the ball rolling. The golden rule is not to act as censor because of hidden preferences.

The next stage is to go through the list and sort out the wheat from the chaff. It needs to be done sensitively because the person who thought of an idea will probably remember saying it although the rest of the group may have forgotten. Then the list can be grouped (for example 'short term, long term, medium term' or 'those that need extra money and help, those which don't'). Or a long list can be turned into a list of priorities once the no-hopers have been weeded out.

### Advantages

- A lot of ideas can be generated in a short time. Groups constantly surprise themselves by discovering how many ways there are of looking at something.
- Instead of concentrating on a few ideas from those people who normally start the discussion, a wider range of people join in.
- Because there is a time lag between a suggestion and its consideration, an idea can be discussed and rejected without anyone losing face.
- Sometimes plans which saw the light of day in a brainstorm but were not used there can be taken away and worked on elsewhere.

### Disadvantages

- The leader must acknowledge all contributions. This may mean time spent on things which wouldn't work or on interesting ideas which are not central to the group's task.
- Sometimes the very wealth of ideas makes the selection of key items difficult.
- People get discouraged and are unlikely to share their thoughts so readily a second time if good ideas are

consistently ignored. Only brainstorm if you really have an open mind about the issues.

*Example*

In planning a mission, having first set out a clear purpose, brainstorms could be used several times, each in relation to one clear topic: What methods could be used to carry it out? (door-to-door leafleting, key speakers, local radio, firework party, healing service, art workshop, etc.) Where is the money coming from? What time and talents are needed? How is prayer to be encouraged? Other churches? Young people?

## 5. Buzz groups

These involve inviting members of a large group to spend a short time talking to one or two people nearby about a specific topic or, more often, to say what they think about what they have just heard. Buzz groups should be short and snappy to catch first reactions without getting involved in a proper debate.

*Advantages*

- When a group has been listening quietly for some time and attention is flagging buzz groups can create a new surge of energy and interest.
- Points of view can be exchanged while they are still fresh.
- People are encouraged to raise their questions in the large group if they discover that others in the buzz group share their problem.
- Ideas and experience can be pooled.
- A personal contact is made in what can otherwise feel like a large impersonal situation.
- It doesn't need any furniture-moving and can be done with a group of any size.
- It allows people to move slightly and stretch.

*Disadvantages*

- There is no time for deep discussion and things can be left tantalizingly in the air.
- People may not listen to each other very well because they are waiting for their chance to say their bit. So the discussion is disorganized and wanders all over the place.
- It may be difficult to hear if you have, for example, 30 people talking at once in the same room.

## 6. Case study

A case study is an account of a concrete situation (true or fictional) in sufficient and credible detail to make it possible for groups to analyse what is going on. The discussion usually allows a wide variety of possible responses. One person may know what has led up to the event in the past few years, another has local knowledge of what is available now, a third has seen this kind of situation before. What might be useful is practical or technical knowledge, time, prayer, a personal contact and so on, and rarely are they combined in one person.

*Advantages*

- Case studies can lead to an understanding of a variety of approaches and skills, demonstrating the scriptural teaching that members of the Body of Christ have different and complementary gifts.
- There is a sense that we are all in this together.

*Disadvantages*

- It can just be an interesting discussion with no clear outcomes. Who in the end does what?

*Example*

Derek and Maria have been married seven years and have two children, Emma aged six and Peter aged three. Their third child was born prematurely at 28 weeks and died seven days later. Both parents spent much of that week at the hospital and the children went to see their sister, taking her drawings and a little present. The chaplain was a great support at the time but he left the day after the child died to go on holiday.

Derek and Maria called themselves Church of England but the parish in which they lived was without any minister as they were waiting for a new appointment. The minister who took the funeral knew there was a pastoral visiting scheme in the parish and arranged for some visits.

The visits seemed to be welcome. It was usually Maria who was seen. She said she was afraid things would never be the same again, she did not know what to tell the children, she felt tired and bad-tempered and hopeless. Above all her relationship with Derek was worse than it had ever been. He did not seem to feel the tragedy the way she did.

Derek was scared Maria was losing her grip. He also wanted to mourn but felt he had to keep going. People kept asking him how Maria was, they never asked about him.

What are the issues facing Derek?

What are the issues facing Maria?

What is the problem from Emma's point of view (and Peter's)?

What are the challenges to the pastoral carers, including practical things like time as well as deep issues such as the meaning of death?

## 7. Demonstration

Learners can either watch a skilled practitioner at work or can be helped to try for themselves – or both.

*Advantages*

- Involvement means that learners can see, hear and possibly touch the learning materials.
- It does not depend on the ability to read.
- Learners can discover where they need further practice before using their skill in the real world.

- Sometimes a demonstration of how not to do something can be very illuminating. People can be encouraged to spot the mistakes and talk afterwards about alternative ways of acting.

*Disadvantages*

- Sometimes a demonstration by an expert can be depressing, leaving the spectator doubting that such skills can ever be learned.
- It can suggest that there is only one correct way of doing something.

*Example*

This might be a demonstration of administering the chalice or reading a lesson in church.

## 8. Group interview

This involves an invitation to someone with expert knowledge and experience to be interviewed by a small group.

*Advantages*

- It is a spontaneous giving of facts and opinions by experts in response to questions of real importance to both sides.
- Subjects can be tackled at greater depth than in a more public setting.
- Time is used economically because the task is clear.
- Sympathy with and understanding of the complexity of issues can be grasped.

*Disadvantages*

- The event can become disorganized without careful planning of the ground to be covered.
- It can be used to sound off against those in authority.

## 9. Group listening

This means listening without interruption or comment to what a person has to say, showing interest without words. It is often used to teach counselling skills but can be used in any group where people are encouraged to say what they really feel and think.

Knowing that you are not going to be interrupted makes a significant difference to what you say. Furthermore, the listeners have no time to rehearse (mentally) what to say when their turn comes because they are giving another person the gift of their total attention. When everyone has finished there is time to reflect on the experience.

The group should be small – five or six maximum – otherwise it is hard to remember, it goes on too long and may be repetitive.

### Advantages

- It is often a revelation to learn what a difference it makes to what you say and how you feel if someone gives you total attention – and how much they appreciate it when you really listen to them.
- It creates a climate of trust.
- It can be used for intimate sharing or as an ice-breaker with a new group.

### Disadvantages

- People can 'cheat' and hog the time (though they rarely do).
- They can say things they may later regret.
- It is difficult to listen when you are tired or uncomfortable, preoccupied or nervous.

### Examples

(a) A Quaker exercise consists of giving people a list of questions from which they choose to answer one. Some of the questions are 'easy', for example, what is your favourite bit of the Bible? Others are deeper: who sat where round the meal table when you were a child and what did it feel like? A timekeeper ensures that everyone is given an equal amount of the group's attention. The list in the hand of the one who starts passes from person to person, each talking while they have the paper in their hand. Each person chooses their own question.

(b) Experiencing how not to listen is also very powerful. Divide the group into pairs and suggest that the person with a birthday earliest in the year is A and the other is B. A must talk on an agreed (easy) topic e.g. 'one of my favourite holidays', for a few minutes. B's task is to sit close by, appearing to listen but in fact, without saying a word, clearly showing lack of interest by winding a watch, looking around the room, fidgeting, etc. When this exercise is done in a large group it is very striking how the noise level plummets. It starts off with half the participants talking with animation. Quite soon it gets quieter as the As dry up because they are missing the tiny non-verbal signs of interest normally given by a listener.

The exercise must be followed by ample time to talk about the experience. Although everyone knows it is 'not real', it is only human to feel a little bit angry or hurt by being ignored. Nor is it easy for the Bs to be so insensitive and they need to talk about that too. And both need to reflect on how they listen and to whom in daily life.

## 10. Fishbowl

This rather alarming word describes a process which can be used in several quite distinct ways. What they have in common is that a small group, part of a larger group, takes part in an activity such as a discussion, while the rest of the group sit apart, perhaps around the edge of the room, observing.

*(a) Fishbowl looking at group process.* The observers sit in silence and must not be tempted to react in any visible or audible way (even gentle laughter or sharp intakes of breath or scraping of chairs), lest they cause a distraction. To watch others without directly participating is a disciplined activity.

The task can be helped by giving observers handouts

before the activity starts (and time to read them!) with some suggestions, questions and checklists.

Some observers can be asked to watch a particular person or group or some aspect of behaviour, such as body language.

Plenty of time must be given to talk this experience through. The purpose of a fishbowl, as with any observation exercise, is to give feedback in such a way as to help the person who receives it to be more effective.

*(b) Fishbowl to focus discussion in a large group* by combining the virtues of both large and small groups. The large group listens to a discussion among a small group drawn from their midst. This may be a better way of spending time than a discussion in the large group itself where it is often difficult for an argument to be pursued. If there is time, the fishbowl can be dissolved and the group can pick up the issues together or in a number of small groups.

*(c) Flexible fishbowl,* leaving one empty space in the fishbowl circle of chairs. Anyone from the outer ring may join at any time, but when they do so, someone already in the fishbowl must leave. It clearly means more people can join in and there has to be some friendly give and take.

*(d) Fishbowl of a sub-group,* made up of people with something in common which is not shared by the rest of the group. It can be experience (of working on the mission field or handling budgets) or a role (curates or incumbents in training parishes) or something intrinsic (women or young people). The listeners may afterwards form their own fishbowl when they too are listened to without interruption. Once again plenty of time must be left for discussion in the group as a whole. It will probably need to be slightly structured.

*Advantages*

- It can provide a rare chance to see yourself as others see you. They are not necessarily right, of course, but they will probably provide food for thought. In practice more people find it harder to believe that they have done something helpful and positive than to believe that what they did was flawed.

- It brings the advantages of a small group discussion to the large group.
- It gives a voice to a minority who may otherwise find it hard to speak.
- On controversial issues it gives time for an uninterrupted statement of a point of view. And the one who disagrees has time to reflect before getting a chance to put an opposing view.

*Disadvantages*

- It takes time.
- It sounds much worse than it is in practice. People often say afterwards how anxious they were at the beginning, but how much they actually learned.
- Some people give feedback which is inaccurate or even unfair. Challenging this needs skilled leadership (though it does not necessarily need to be done by the leader himself).
- It is very hard for some people to sit quietly without getting involved in the discussion.
- It needs skilled, experienced leadership.

## 11. Ice-breakers

These open a learning programme with four purposes in mind:

to help participants get to know each other;
to create a friendly and co-operative climate;
to discover what mixture of experience, attitudes and knowledge there is in the group;
to create an interest right from the start both in the topic and the way it is going to be learned.

*Advantages*

- It saves time because a lot of information can be got across quickly.
- It creates a 'place of safety' from the beginning, just

when people are wondering what sort of group they have joined and what sort of event they have let themselves in for.

- It establishes the style of the event which is going to include active not passive learning.
- It can be great fun.

### Disadvantages

- Done clumsily it can be intrusive. No one should be asked to disclose any information or feelings they do not wish to share. The approach must be thought through with sensitivity.
- Some people can feel overwhelmed by a lot of new experiences.

### Examples

(a) Simple introduction by every member of a group, perhaps name; where they have come from; why they have come; job (but does this put those not in paid employment at a disadvantage?); one thing they hope to get out of the meeting; one thing they fear might happen.

(b) Divide the group into pairs, ask them to introduce themselves to each other and then ask each to introduce the other to the larger group.

(c) Ask everyone to bring one object to the group and say why it is important to them.

(d) Depending on the bravery of the leader, the name game can be played. The person sitting next to the leader is asked to say her name. The person sitting next to her says her name too, followed by 'Hello Susie'. Person three introduces himself and then says hello to the two previous people in turn and by name. This continues round the group and the hapless leader goes last, with, of course, the longest list of names to remember.

## 12. Medium X

This involves anything from a video tape to interactive computer-based material.

*Advantages*

- A great deal of effort and expertise can be compressed into one package and it can be used again and again.
- It ensures that everyone has the same quality learning experience.
- It has all the advantages of open learning materials, especially the ability to make progress at one's own pace.
- Concentration and motivation may be stimulated by such things as recorded role play, demonstrations and documentaries.

*Disadvantages*

- The novelist and academic Umberto Eco said 'If you want to use television to teach somebody something, you first have to teach somebody how to use television'.
- It may mean substantial initial expenditure and the radical reorganization of teaching techniques.
- It raises important issues about who is in charge of the learning process since the package is a 'given'. Even in interactive material the options available are not chosen by the learner.
- It is possible to get carried away and stray into side issues.
- Access to equipment may be difficult for some. Even in households with videos, the rest of the family may have priority demands.
- Unless it is kept short and combined with ways of responding, it destroys the point of the group. If people watch a video for half an hour or more their memory of what they saw and ability to respond will be reduced.

### 13. On-the-job training

The trainee is actively involved in performing a real but unfamiliar task followed by time to reflect with the trainer and possibly with others. Sometimes journals are kept but in any case there is a systematic attempt to learn from what happens.

*Advantages*

- The difficulties and delights of the job are encountered while there is time to talk them over and possibly take action.
- A real job is being done.
- The trainee develops habits of reflecting on and learning from experience.
- It keeps the trainer in touch with the practicalities of the job.

*Disadvantages*

- It can be seen and resented as informal assessment.
- It takes time, since although the trainer may not need to be present, plans have to be made and permissions sought. And the trainee must be properly briefed.
- Trainees can seek out those who confirm bad habits.
- The reflection process can be skimped so that 'experience' is not turned into learning, but is justified as an end in itself.

### 14. Open learning

Open learning is not the same as distance learning. It can be done at a distance but can also happen in a crowded room. It means that the learner is working alone at a comfortable pace on prepared materials and has more choice and control than in many other methods. Sometimes 'open learning' refers to access to courses, sometimes to choice about which part of the course or subject is studied, sometimes to where, when and how the study is done.

*Advantages*

- It cuts out wasted time, as learners can skip or skim quickly over what they already know or what is irrelevant.
- There is more choice and control: learning can be fitted in to the demands of work or home.
- Difficult or important parts can be referred to again and again as and when needed.
- Many people can benefit from a single package, which may include audio tapes, video recordings, computer software.
- It can be mixed with live sessions.
- It can reach you wherever you live.

*Disadvantages*

- Most of the benefits of learning with other people are lost, such as sharing information, enthusiasm and experience, discussion and debating, and being able to act together to change things.
- Good quality open learning materials backed by effective learner support have not been easy to come by in the churches, though the situation is improving.

*Examples*

This book.
The Open University, The National Extension College and many courses run by theological colleges and other colleges of Higher Education.

## 15. Portfolio

It describes a collection of work which demonstrates a person's ability and achievements; this can include essays, drawings, diagrams, records of visits or projects or conversations.

*Advantages*

- It starts from a person's experience and builds on their strengths. From the onset it encourages the learner to identify and accept that they already have knowledge and experience which can now be demonstrated.

- It recognizes that experience itself is not enough. The person must also demonstrate that what has been claimed as being learned is now being used.
- By clearly mapping what has already been learned, gaps can be identified so that attention shifts to further learning needs and opportunities, and so the cycle continues, based as it is on the premise that learning is a lifelong process.

*Disadvantages*

- Skilled help, time and imagination are needed at the beginning to build up the learner's confidence.
- Consultation and negotiation are needed to continue the process lest it gets out of hand (everything gets included) or dries up (through lack of time, despair at how much one doesn't know, or the impossibility of doing anything about the further training needs which have been identified).
- The key is individual motivation and the assumption that people have the energy and resources to plan, reflect and be self-directing. Its very strengths – the encouragement of investigative, analytical and creative tasks, needing independent judgement and self-awareness – mean that not everyone can do this at all times in their lives.

*Example*

The Open University has produced *A Portfolio Approach to Personal and Career Development* (E530) which can be used either as a short course by an individual or, for a higher fee, with tutor and counselling support for assessment and accreditation.

### 16. Problem-solving session

This is based on drawing out the creativity and skills in the group, using a four-fold process:

an experience-based exercise to get people interested in the problem;

a talk setting out some factors or opinions about the subject;

a reminder of how we naturally set about tackling problems;

an exercise using the imagination to help see the problem in a new hopeful way.

*Advantages*

- This method is particularly useful where a group has a common purpose and problem.
- It uses everyone's ideas.
- It builds up relationships.
- It teaches people a way of thinking about problems which they can use in other situations.

*Disadvantages*

- Some people may be alarmed at the unusual approach. It works best with a group who have said they are willing to have a go.
- A great many ideas are likely to be generated and this is overwhelming and confusing for some.
- The leader needs to know a little about the theory of problem-solving (and about the matter under discussion).
- The leader must genuinely want people to do their own thinking and must not have a cherished solution ready prepared, which is going to be adopted despite everyone else.

*Example*

The subject is leadership. Scripture is read: many gifts in the one Body (Romans 12.4–8).

*Part 1* – one half of the room is asked to talk about what makes for good leadership and the rest tackles what makes for poor leadership. They talk in pairs and are asked to recall their own experience of both leading and being led, and without recording personal details, to pull out from that the main features. These are recorded on flip-chart paper, mainly as single words or phrases.

*Part 2* – a short talk on what makes a good leader: God's grace? the ability you were born with? intelligence and competency? a certain attitude which takes risks and is passionate? experience? being in the right place at the right time? prayerful support from others? clear structures and responsibilities?

*Part 3* – a description of the various stages of problem-solving: exploration and mapping; generation of ideas; commitment (within each there is an imaginative expansive phase when judgement is suspended, followed by convergence and closure).

*Part 4* – think of a problem in connection with your own leadership or that exercised in the group by someone else. Write it down in one sentence. Then the leader reads out the following sentences leaving people time to complete each in turn:

> This is important to me because . . .
> An alternative way of putting it is . . .
> However the main point is . . .
> But what I would really like to do is . . .
> If only I could break all the laws of reality I would . . .
> Put another way the problem could be likened to . . .
>    (find a metaphor)
> It sounds to me like a problem to do with . . .
> Putting it all together it seems that what has to be done
>    is . . .

Finally people are asked to indicate if their final sentence differs significantly from their first.

The exercise can be done in small groups (up to four) instead of individually. Some people will enjoy the exercise greatly. If others are stuck, they can be helped by suggesting they just change one word in their original sentence and reflect on that before going further.

*Part 5* – plan some action!

## 17. Project/visit

This is 'homework' done before or between or after other sessions. It may include almost anything and can be tackled by people alone (asking neighbours what they think the church is for) or by a group (a visit to a day centre) or by a congregation (a visit to another church). It is done with a purpose as part of something else and there is always time to look back on it and tease out what can be learned from the experience.

*Advantages*

- Students are invited to explore new situations in a spirit of enquiry or look again at things which are familiar.
- A group visit or project provides the opportunity to learn in co-operation rather than in competition.
- Such experience can reinforce or build on what is being learned in more formal sessions.
- The possibilities are only limited by the imagination of the leader.

*Disadvantages*

- It requires extra time and energy for planning – phone calls, letters, meetings perhaps.
- Instructions must be clear to avoid the disappointment that will be felt if through a misunderstanding the wrong task is carried out.
- It takes time, not least the reflection afterwards (though this is often where significant learning takes place).

## 18. Reporting-back session

This is a method of helping a large group hear something of what has taken place in its constituent small groups or symposia.

*Advantages*

- Different issues can be tackled at the same time by small groups who chose their particular subject but have an interest in others.
- A large number of ideas can be pooled.
- Curiosity is satisfied.
- People are helped to feel they belong to the whole event, not just to their small group.

*Disadvantages*

- It can be monumentally boring and repetitive if each group feels it has a right to the same 'air-time'.
- The need to report back can be elevated into the main task of the small group so the issues get lost and all the effort goes into making a good presentation.

*Examples*

(a) Ask each group to select their three most important points. Go round each group in turn asking for their first point only. If their first has already been covered by another group they go on to their second or third. No point needs to be repeated.

(b) Give each group a sheet of flip-chart paper and ask them to record their findings. They can use lists, pictures, cartoons, devise a postcard with a message, etc. The sheets are then put on display and the whole group mills around looking at each in turn. This can be followed first by questions for clarification, then general discussion.

(c) If people have worked alone or in pairs, it is impossible to receive all the ideas. 'Best points' can be written on Post-it stickers and stuck on flip-chart paper. Prepare a sheet of paper (or sheets) so that certain subjects can be grouped under agreed headings. This makes the wealth of ideas easier to handle.

(d) Allow a certain amount of time for each group to report back (be strict) and suggest different ways of getting their message across: an impromptu sketch, mime, drawings, giant postcards, quizzes and much, much more.

## 19. Role play

Volunteers are asked to ad lib their way through a 'sketch'. A typical scene is described in outline – a teenager coming home late to her family or a Church Council faced with a tricky decision. People should be given parts which are not like their real-life situations: lay people role-play the clergy and vice versa, older people can take younger parts and even gender roles can be reversed. Characters may be given simple instructions (father usually hides behind newspaper and likes a quiet life; new church treasurer is very optimistic about raising giving in the next year, etc.). Then it is up to the 'cast' to make it up as they go along for a few minutes.

The beginning and the end need to be clearly marked so that participants know when they are in role and at what point they are 'released' to become themselves again. There must be ample time to talk about what happened so that learning at many levels can take place.

There are several variations:

(a) Instead of keeping the same people in role all the time, new actors can replace them. This works only when there are few characters and the task is clear, such as responding to a Sunday School teacher who is unsuitable.

(b) Before you start ask two or three people to volunteer to play a part and ask all except one to leave the room. They are called in one at a time to give the group a chance to see how different people handle the same problem.

(c) Alternatively role play can be done in pairs or threes and fours. Then all the group is divided up and the role play is done at the same time by everyone. There is less acting – simply a question of drawing chairs together in a spot where noises off will not be distracting. In groups of three or more there can be an observer, e.g. a couple with a problem come to see a minister and the fourth member listens and watches both what is said and unsaid. This may be followed by discussion within the small group first, then the whole group.

*Advantages*

- Role play not only provokes thought but also helps people to reflect on their feelings. It reaches parts no passive learning can reach.
- It gives a chance to practise skills.
- It can be great fun.
- It gives a group a chance to get to know each other, particularly when they explain that they are not really like that.
- Some people find that playing a role and saying things they would not normally say, e.g., being more assertive than usual or very much quieter, helps them to understand themselves more.
- It can be better than many discussion groups at making the point simply and clearly that there is more than one way of looking at things or tackling a problem. Time and again people remark that they are impressed with how much experience and wisdom are locked in a group (and in themselves) and rarely seen.

*Disadvantages*

- It needs experienced leadership. Sometimes raw feelings emerge when the sketch inadvertently touches on a real-life painful situation. It may remind people of past experiences they would rather forget.
- The follow-up discussion has to be done according to clear guidelines so that people can learn how others see them. It can be devastating if someone sees you as 'weak' when you were trying to role-play a patient and caring person. Such a remark has to be followed by exploring what 'weak' means to the speaker – and what it means to be 'strong' in the situation.
- On the other hand it can be so enjoyable that it needs firm leadership to keep the group to the task in hand.

## 20. Sculpting

A group performs a role play. When it ends, instead of discussion, a volunteer from the audience walks up to the 'actors' and in silence arranges them in a tableau. Thus the group has a picture of how one person sees the inter-action which has taken place, for example, who was central to the group, who was an outsider, who calls the tune, who keeps their head down hoping it will all go away...

The observing group then discuss their view of what went on. Next the actors are asked to resume their seats and give their views. For example, did they feel as dominant or isolated as the tableau suggests?

*Advantages*

- This is a very powerful way of learning that people have different perceptions of what is happening and that, far from bringing conflict, our differences – if we listen – can teach us a great deal.
- Some people find it fun too.

*Disadvantages*

- A skilled and experienced leader is necessary.
- Sculpting has to be introduced at the right time to gain most benefit.
- Some people dislike such participatory methods.

*Example*

A role play lasting five to ten minutes depicts mother, father, teenage son and grandmother reacting to teenage daughter who comes home late/failed to come home at all the previous night. The first observer could place the 'daughter' standing on a chair in the centre to show how her absence/presence dominates the rest of the family. The son might be on the edge of the group facing outwards. Or perhaps one of the parents is seen as central. Different people pick up different clues as to what is going on and so together can contribute to a pool of understanding.

## 21. Simulation

This is a recreation of a real-life setting which is likely to be encountered after training. It has three stages: briefing, action and evaluation.

## Advantages

- It helps people explore their reaction to a situation before they face the real thing.
- If the task is complicated it can be broken up into more manageable bits and these tackled one at a time.

## Disadvantages

- Some people are impatient with pretence and cannot function normally in an unreal situation.

## Example

In a session on building up the community of men and women in the Church, men and women sit at opposite sides of the room. The women are then asked to walk thoughtfully across the room and select one of the men with whom she would have a ten-minute conversation on the topic. Each pair then talks about what it feels like to choose and be chosen.

It emerged that the women felt uncomfortable about making a choice which of necessity meant they were excluding others. Men felt it was strange not to be taking the initiative. They felt quite helpless. Together they came to a deeper understanding of the constraints both sexes operate under.

## 22. Symposium

A panel of speakers present different points of view on a chosen topic to an audience who are probably given an opportunity to question them. Each member of the panel may be given a few minutes to express their views before questions are asked.

## Advantages

- Contrasting views stimulate thought and give the listeners a chance to discover or confirm their own ideas.
- A great deal of experience and knowledge can be tapped quickly.

- The brevity of the contributions and the variety of voices and personalities prevents interest from flagging.

## Disadvantages

- The audience is fairly helpless if things do not go according to plan.
- The whole panel can get off the subject (or never really get on it).
- The personality of a speaker may overshadow the content of what is said.
- Some vocal speakers or questioners may monopolize the session. It can be tedious and repetitive if each speaker is expected to reply to every question.

## 23. Talk/lecture/sermon

A prepared talk gives information, generates understanding and creates interest by using a clear structure, reasoned argument, relevant examples, illustrations and summaries. It may be accompanied by visual aids such as handouts, blackboards, flip charts, overhead projectors, slides and models.

The beginning is important because attention is high. Try not to start with apologies. Tried and tested openings are: describe 'coming attractions' or highlights of the lecture, pose a question for the listeners to mull over while you talk, tell a subject-related story.

Key words to summarize the main points are helpful. So too are real-life illustrations. Keep linking the material to the experience the listeners already have.

## Variations

Audience interest can be held in a number of ways:

**Pre-talk preparation.** If there is time, arrange to collect questions on the subject beforehand, then build the talk around them. It is the best way of making sure you are reaching the target. If questions are asked for and then ignored in the talk, there may be trouble.

***Question list.*** The speaker sends on ahead a list of questions, more than could be tackled in the talk. The audience or congregation is asked to select the most important. Even if the response is late or never properly completed, the questions themselves generate interest so that people come to the event having done some thinking beforehand.

***Buzz groups.*** Attention can be improved by breaking the lecture up with activities for learners like buzz groups.

***Stop and start.*** Interrupt the lecture from time to time to give people a chance to reflect and make notes.

***Skeleton outline.*** Before you start, distribute a brief outline of what you intend to say, set out with plenty of space for added notes.

***Quizzes.*** Hand out a simple quiz which will only take a few minutes to answer. Make it as user-friendly as possible and follow it with several possibilities, only one of which should be circled. Or make a list of statements and ask people to mark each 'F' for false and 'T' for true; for example, an Anglican clergyman is legally bound to conduct weddings for everyone who lives in his or her parish who has not previously been married. Encourage the audience to have a go at answering the quiz even if they may get some things wrong. The answers do not need to be shown to anyone since they are not a test, just designed to get the brain up and running before the start. Then build the talk in such a way as to answer the questions as you go along.

***Guess and test.*** Perhaps the questions are open-ended and have no 'right' answer. Again encourage listeners to put down what they think. After the talk they can consider alone or in pairs or with the speaker whether their opinion has changed.

***Silence.*** Follow a talk by giving listeners the chance to work out the implications for them in their daily lives. Silence after a sermon can be very powerful. Or questions can be suggested: Which ideas were new for you? Which ring bells?

Which apply to your situation at home or at work? Do you need to plan to do anything as a result?

***Question-time.*** Announce that the speaker can be asked questions at the end. Such question-time can, alas, be hijacked by one or two people for their own ends. It is striking how often the first question sets the tone for the rest.

***Horseshoes.*** Arrange all the chairs in a horseshoe shape with the open end facing the speaker. You then have ready-made small groups with very little disturbance and can intersperse talk with assimilation of ideas in groups as and when appropriate.

***Cabaret.*** Arrange chairs in groups of three or four, with or without a table, cabaret style. Overall the pattern may be nearly circular. Try having the speaker in the corner if it makes more space.

### Advantages

- Any method known to have been used for 2,500 years is likely to be effective.
- It is economical because it can reach a large number of people and the same material can be used more than once.
- A nervous tutor who could not handle a wide-ranging discussion can be persuaded to teach by being given time to prepare a limited subject well.
- Although the content may be mostly forgotten, there may be long-term gains: new insights or new motivation to read about, think or discuss the ideas.
- Done well, it is irreplaceable.

### Disadvantages

- It asks of the audience sustained, passive listening. People differ in their ability not only to do that but also to want to do it.
- We are more and more used to having our fancy tickled by variety and novelty. The media accustom us to captions and slogans rather than reasoned argument.

- It is not as effective as small-group discussion for complex problem-solving or for changing attitudes.
- Even in imparting ideas and information, after 20 minutes there is a marked decline in attention followed by a peak just before the lecture ends.
- One problem for lecturers is that they rarely get a chance to learn how effective (or ineffective) they have been. As there are not likely to be end-of-term exams, it is possible for the belief that real learning is taking place to go unchallenged for years.
- The disadvantages are best illustrated by a game:

One-way communication . . .
A volunteer stands in front of a group and tells members how to draw a particular pattern of squares. The instruction should begin with the top square and describe each one in turn. The group must draw in silence, not asking questions. The results are discussed.

Two-way communication . . .
Then the same person repeats the exercise with a different pattern of figures, but this time anyone can ask questions, including getting the instructions repeated as often as necessary. The results are compared with the first drawing. It is likely that the second set is markedly more accurate.

## 24. Visual sessions

Visual material can be used not just to illustrate talks but as a means of learning in itself.

*Advantages*

- Pictures reach parts words cannot reach.
- Whether or not members can read English is irrelevant.

*Disadvantages*

- Careful preparation is necessary. Pictures from magazines, photographs, or postcards, need to be collected, often from a number of sources, and they should relate

directly to the task in hand. They wear out and so need
to be replaced.

- Some people feel this is not 'real' learning, only play.

*Examples*

(a) If you want to divide a large group into smaller ones
in a way that will mix them up but also start to build
relationships, have enough copies of several pictures made
so that each person in the group can have one. Mix all the
pictures up and scatter them round the room. Participants
then choose one and go to a pre-arranged place to meet
the other people who chose the same picture (put one
copy on the door to mark the space).

(b) Scatter pictures on a table and ask everyone to choose
one. Have plenty so there is real choice even for those who
find it hard to make up their mind. Discuss in pairs and in
the group. Postcards from art galleries of how various artists
have painted Christ can stimulate a discussion of
Christology.

(c) Members are given a number of magazines and papers
and asked to cut out anything which makes them think of
justice and injustice. They then work as a group on a collage
which can be used to show to others their concerns.

## 25. Workshops

This is a group event which may include seminars or lectures but which is set up so that each member actively
participates. The outcome – which is to be able to do
something better than before – depends at least as much
on what participants learn from each other as from the
planned input.

*Advantages*

- Participants are given a chance to try new ways of learning, particularly a more open-ended approach.
- To have something to contribute to an event is an
encouraging feeling and makes it more likely that
people will build on what they have learned.

- There is a wide cross-fertilization of ideas and experience.
- Co-leading a workshop with an expert in the field is a good way of developing one's own abilities.
- There is some freedom to learn at one's own pace and in one's own way.

*Disadvantages*

- Unless clear information and objectives are set out in advance, people may come prepared to be passive learners and to listen to a series of talks. They can be resentful and disruptive when they find they are expected to take part.
- Planning and preparation take a great deal of time.
- Careful planning with the person on site is also needed.
- Skilled, experienced leadership is necessary. Never work as co-leader with someone at short notice if you have not worked with them before.
- With so much going on time can be a problem. If sessions start late or overrun their agreed slot, some people will feel unsettled. Better to allow a proper coffee break and start again punctually than have a session with a ragged beginning.
- If the group is large (over 20), it can be difficult to feel part of the whole event. It may be more comfortable to be in the small group and reporting-back sessions may be repetitive and dull or competitive and anxiety-provoking.

# 6

## Putting It All Together

This chapter has four sections:

A.  *Educational foundations: aims, objectives and outcomes*
    How to distinguish between all three and understand their usefulness to the learner, the tutor and the 'sponsors'.
B.  *Counting the cost*
    Ten clusters of questions, useful for gathering information when starting to plan.
C.  *A plan of action*
    How to shape a good design.
D.  *Some common pitfalls*

### A. Educational foundations: aims, objectives and outcomes

#### Aims

An *aim* is a general statement about the direction in which you want to go. Aims are easy to write. Some call them 'motherhood and apple pie' statements because no one in their right mind would disagree with them. One clearly focused sentence should contain the lot. Complicated clauses simply store up trouble. For example, this chapter *aims* to help you design events and programmes more effectively.

A church may have a medium or long-term *aim*: 'to deepen the prayer life of the congregation and the individuals within it'; or 'to increase membership and participation by virtue of a campaign in the neighbourhood in a year's time'; or 'to make church members and local leaders aware of how the church hall could be better used'.

Or the *aim* of a single evening may be, 'to help people realize the benefits of a Lent course', or 'to persuade people to help run sessions for confirmation candidates'.

## Objectives

*Objectives* tell you *how* the task is going to be tackled. Clearly any plan chosen is not the only way the aim could have been tackled. Objectives mean making choices, judging what is feasible in the circumstances and knowing that other good options have to be neglected. Because they are more limited than aims, there are more of them. They break the aim down into manageable parts. An objective is a clear statement of what you intend to do. It tells where you are going and how to get there. It describes to the learner what they can reasonably expect to have learned by the end.

### Making objectives work for the learner

Objectives:

- can be set out in the publicity designed to recruit learners or in a handout at the meeting; written up when everyone is there or simply spoken at the beginning;
- show learners what they are to do, alerting them to challenges and giving them an idea not only of the area to be covered but of the process used in getting there, for example talks by experts, homework, group work, etc.;
- show learners what they have achieved as they go along, thus building up confidence to go a further step;
- show learners what they have yet to master and what the problem areas might be, so they are not surprised and discouraged when they encounter them;
- show learners why they are being asked to do things, how they fit into the total plan;
- allow the learner to use the experience for accreditation if that is an option.

*Making objectives work for those putting on the course*

Objectives:

- describe to someone who has not been present what is happening and what is likely to be learnt;
- bring in accountability which may challenge them to learn from experience and rethink priorities or extend the work to another area.

*Making objectives work for the teacher*

Objectives help the teacher to check that what is planned is:

- relevant to what needs to be learned;
- attainable by those for whom it is designed;
- feasible, i.e., there are the skills, resources and time to do what they say they are going to do;
- evaluated so as to learn from each event.

## Outcomes

*Outcomes* are the desired changes in thought and action made as a result of undertaking some educational or training programme. There has recently been a tendency to concentrate on the outcome of courses rather than their aims and objectives. The latter are, after all, aspirations and hopes. And they focus on the journey as well as on the arrival.

Outcomes are more concrete and more measurable. They are often linked to competencies: can this person do what is required or not? And in the secular world funding is likely to follow evidence of competency. They present a timely reminder that learning should change the way we are and the world we live in. But too narrow a focus on outcomes is restrictive.

### B. *Counting the cost*

This is a checklist for people thinking of running a wide range of training events: for example a house church course, a confirmation class, a Lent group, a church week-

end, an event for Sunday School leaders or youth workers,
leader training.

## *Is the proposed event needed?*

Who is asking for it?
Is there a demand already there or do we need to create
  a demand which does not yet exist?
Is it really necessary? Why is it being offered?
Who is it for?
Who do we need to get permission from?

## *Who is going to run it?*

Who knows about this area?
Who has done it before? How did it work?
Can we do it ourselves or do we need someone to help?
From whom can we get help and advice?
Has the person chosen got time to do it?
Does it need more than one person? If so how will a
  team be built? Who will head the team?
Does someone need to be in charge of hospitality?
If someone comes from outside what do they need to
  know about the subject and about the people who
  are coming?
Who will do the briefing?

## *What will it cost?*

Who will pay any expenses?
Do we make a charge? Should there be a sliding scale
  or voluntary donations? (It is often found that
  people are more likely to turn up if they have paid
  something, however little.)
Can people be asked to buy pamphlets, etc.?
Is there a minimum number needed to cover the cost?
Should travel costs be pooled?

## *Where will it be held?*

At home or away?
How many rooms/what size/kitchen or catering/how

easy to find it/reasonably comfortable chairs/
heating/lighting/parking/public transport/crèche
facilities/wheelchair access?

### Who are we aiming at?

A group already existing or a new one?
An open group or one for particular people, for example
Church Council members, parents?
What is the best size? (As a general rule, the larger the
event, the more expertise is needed.)

### When will it be held?

How long will it last? Morning/afternoon/evening/
overnight?
What else might help or hinder? School holiday/
weekday/festival?
What else is going on then? In other parts of the parish,
in other churches, the deanery, the community,
diocese?
At what times is it best to travel?
How much time will people be prepared to give?

### Is equipment needed?

Books, projector, tape player, video recorder, etc.?
Does someone know how they work?
Is there a handy plug or an extension lead?
Flip chart, pens, paper, Blu-tack, display board?
Is it forbidden to put anything on the walls?

### How do we invite people?

What do they read already? Parish notice sheet? Vicar's
letter? Community newsletter? Free newspaper?
Church notice board? Small ads in the library,
supermarket, fish and chip shop?
What else will they read? Leaflet for the congregation?
Personal invitation? Door-to-door mailing?
Who has skills in publicity and communications? Could
they help?

How can word-of-mouth be encouraged?

*What needs sending out beforehand?*

Map? Travel directions?
List of members so they can share travel?
Something which helps us find out what they know
   already, what they want to learn and what skills and
   experience they bring to the event?

*What can we learn from the event?*

Will we offer participants a chance to tell us what they
   learned and found useful, either at the end or, say,
   three to six months later?
Will those who run the event meet together to assess
   how far it met its targets and what were the
   unforeseen gains and losses?
How can the staff help each other to reflect on their
   strengths and weaknesses, and to learn from that?
   (Misunderstandings to avoid, more rest, more training
   to develop a gift?)

## C. *A plan of action*

### Designing the event

*Brainstorm* all the ways ahead which you might use: people,
places, times, methods, resources.

*Outline:* sort out the individual stages: start by building
interest and whetting the appetite.
   Provide variety:

easy/hard sessions;
sometimes the learner is active, at other times passive;
work alone or in pairs or a small group or all together.

Break hard things down into simpler bits. Put them in
order and test them against your aim and objectives. Does
it make a balanced whole?
   Some people use a rule of thirds for an event which lasts
a day or longer:

- fully programme the first third;
- lightly programme the second third;
- leave the last third fairly unprogrammed at least with regard to content (allows participants to inject ideas).

Include a 'so what?' session: for example, where do we go from here? what difference does all this make to my daily life or the life of the congregation or the neighbourhood or the nation?

Evaluation is essential and need not take long. Owning up to the parts you as organizer felt went wrong can be a help. Try not to rush the end.

### Detail:

How long will each part take?
Who is doing what? When are they doing it?
Who will explain to those taking part what is needed?

Collect the resources. Be painstaking: 'For want of a nail the battle was lost.'

**Your own unique contribution.** Do you believe in the plan? If so, trust it, a lot of thought and work has gone into it. It is the best plan available so far. Be prepared to adjust if necessary.

Learn from every experience, even those which fall flat. 'Failures' may tell us more than 'successes'.

Trust the group and the other people involved. You are all in it together.

### D. *Some common pitfalls*

#### *Starting late*

Make it clear exactly when you are going to start. Begin on time with something useful, even if it is not exactly how you had planned to start. If you wait for latecomers, those already there may begin to get restive and may themselves feel free to turn up late at another session.

### Writing on a flip chart

Think which sheets could be prepared beforehand.
Ask someone else to write while you receive responses.
Only record what is necessary.
Trendy colours may not be very visible.

### Reporting back

See entry in Chapter 5.

### Giving confusing information

It is hard to take in details, especially at the beginning
when people are not clear what are the important bits to
remember. For example, write out the timetable and put it
where everyone can see it so they know when worship/
discussion/coffee, etc. is coming. For some people this is
the difference between being in a garden which someone
cares for and being in a wilderness.

### Waiting for volunteers

Give people notice beforehand. Say 'I shall be asking later
for . . . Could you think about this?'

Don't use the time of the full group to organize lifts
home. Ask someone beforehand to receive offers of and
requests for transport.

Divide people into groups or pairs by putting people with
the same birthday months together. If someone has to start,
ask who next has a birthday. People on joining can be given
at random a piece of coloured ribbon or wool or a picture
and asked to go to the table where a similar object is
displayed.

If it's a lunchtime meeting, have enough food for one
person on a plate on each chair. Arrange the chairs in
huddles of an appropriate size. Choosing a plate with a ham
sandwich and a banana takes the strain out of choosing a
group (or being chosen by them).

# 7

# Learning in Groups

This chapter has four sections:

A. *Four basic concerns*
   When any group meets there are basic concerns which need to be addressed.
B. *The distinction between content and process*
C. *Three group tasks:* meeting task, maintenance and individual needs
D. *Group leadership:* different types and functions with suggestions for handling some tricky situations

## A. *Four basic concerns*

The work of Jack Gibb, published in 1964, has been used by the General Synod Board of Education as part of its training programme for the past 30 years. It is based on observation of groups in a wide variety of settings, not all of them educational. It suggests that all groups of human beings share at least four basic concerns, and that if the group takes the time to work out the answers to the questions below, it will be more productive, efficient and enjoyable.

**The four basic concerns are:**

*1. Who am I?*

Who am I in this group at this moment?
Do I have a right to be here? For example, do I know enough?

Have I had the right experience?
What do I do to be accepted in this group?
What does it mean to be a man/woman here?

*If this is unresolved, there will be fear and mistrust in the group.*

## 2. Who are you?

Who are these other people?
What do I need to know about them in order to be able
to trust them?
What do they need to know about me so that we can
work together, share ideas, own up to our mistaken
ideas, get over our failures?

*If this is unresolved, the group will be cautious, members will
be too polite to say what they mean and find it hard to make
decisions or join in activities.*

## 3. What are we here for?

Are we all working for the same thing?
Is this the event I thought it was going to be?
Is it worth doing?
Will it be better or worse than I imagined?
Are the other people here willing to back it?

*If this is unresolved, members may become competitive or sink
into apathy (and probably not come back).*

## 4. How are we going to do it?

Who is in charge? Are they worth my trust and my time?
What are the ways of doing things in this group?
How are we going to get ourselves organized?
How is what is going on outside the group affecting what
we do?

*If this is unresolved, there may be hidden struggles for power or
members may simply let others get on with it (and probably not
come back).*

## B. *The distinction between content and process*

*Content* refers to the actual words that are spoken; *process* is all the rest, seen and unseen. Part of it is what can be observed, how the words were said, gestures, who was there and where they were sitting, whether they looked as if they were paying attention or not, who talked to whom, who interrupted, whether any young people spoke and so on.

Some process can only be sensed and needs to be checked to discover if it only exists in our imagination. Into this area fall members' unspoken feelings, attitudes and concerns, which may have a strong impact on the group. For example, everyone may be feeling new and helpless, assuming that the other people present know each other and will know what to say and do. An unusually silent member may feel she is contributing nothing but may be seen as the most powerful member of the group. A talkative member wants to be friendly and helpful but is seen by some as bossy. The only way of discovering about hidden process is to ask and to share.

What is certain is that

- there always is process in a group, it is not an optional extra.
- process affects content (the medium is the message).
- sometimes when process is unrecognized, it can be disabling.
- prayer can be a powerful intervention in process terms, not always to the good. With or without quotations from Scripture or from authoritative sources it can be used to stifle discussion or to make a point which cannot be 'answered'.

Sometimes we cannot hear what people are saying because their voice is drowned by their actions. For example, I attended a university lecture on communication as part of a Postgraduate Diploma in Adult Education. The topic was one-way communication and we were told that 20 minutes is the limit of most people's attention span, with peaks at the beginning and the end. The lecture lasted for an uninterrupted hour and 50 minutes . . .

## C. *Three group tasks*

### 1. Task needs

- a clear and worthwhile goal
- a plan of action to achieve the goal
- a way of recognizing when the goal has been reached

### 2. Individual needs

Every person there will have some of the following needs:

- to be recognized
- to be accepted
- to feel valued
- to feel their ideas and efforts matter
- to feel useful and have a sense of purpose
- to achieve what they set out to do
- to use their talents

### 3. Maintenance needs

These needs are less well understood. The group itself has a need to stick together until the learning task is done. It must help members co-operate but not at the expense of avoiding conflict which is often a useful gate-keeper to further understanding. Members need to support each other even when disagreeing.

*The strength and life of a group depends on recognizing each of these three sets of needs and attending to them as and when appropriate.*
Sometimes (before a deadline?) the task is all important. Sometimes a member brings a personal need which for a time takes priority (an upsetting experience on the way to the class). Sometimes the group itself needs more tender loving care (a coffee break; a change of venue; negotiation about future plans) before it can get on with the task.

*When* **maintenance** *dominates:* a group learning about parenting young children seems to the facilitator to be wasting time. Classes end later and later. The facilitator raises the problem somewhat reluctantly for it is a very happy and useful group. A solution is reached which pleases everyone: in future the class ends after an hour and a half. If after that anyone wants to stay and talk, there is space for them to do so. In other words, the maintenance needs of the group had threatened to swamp the task. By separating them out, the task was not lost as it might have been had the facilitator decided enough was enough and given up the class because she wanted to see more of her own family.

**When task *dominates:*** a group decides to opt for a course which leads to accreditation. This is an excellent decision for some. But it is achieved at a cost: conflicting opinions are not brought out into the open and resolved. Most of the group was silent. In this case the task needs washed away maintenance and individual needs. It may have been very understandable – perhaps there was an external deadline – but the price may be paid in the future by members not backing the decision or by dropping out.

## D. *Leadership . . . for everyone?*

In a learning situation, leaders are likely to be those who can hold these three functions together and not be too bossy (task-orientated) or over-friendly (concentrating only on individual needs to the neglect of everything else). Such leaders are often described as facilitators because they prepare, draw out, support, co-ordinate and encourage group members in their learning task. These considerations are equally important for those who chair committees and meetings, though the task will be more dominant in these situations.

But an important insight is the recognition that if you list the things leaders do, most are no different from what all group members should do. Everyone can help the learning process in a group by taking on some of the tasks listed below. This is not the same thing as rotating leadership which often fails because it feels insecure and no one person is mindful of the group between sessions.

Groups need people who will

- make new members feel welcome;
- propose tasks or actions;

- bring to the group background information (for example press cuttings) and materials to help with discussion;
- help to organize the best possible layout of the room;
- offer ideas and suggestions;
- ask other group members for ideas and suggestions;
- ask questions;
- listen carefully and link or contrast ideas where possible;
- get people to explore differences and to be reconciled over disagreements;
- admit mistakes;
- avoid criticism of individuals (present or absent) so that no one feels ridiculed or put down;
- be sensitive to different denominations, backgrounds, interests and attitudes;
- break the tension at the right moment by humour which is not unkind;
- draw in those who may feel left out;
- challenge what is said or planned to make sure it is practicable or fits the facts;
- help the group to work out what is causing any problems it might have and what to do about them;
- remind the group of its achievements and inspire it to build on them;
- summarize from time to time where the group has got to;
- sense when the group needs to move on and possibly 'fly a kite' to see which way the wind is blowing;
- join in the evaluation so that the event itself can be a source of learning.

All this is easier said than done!

You might like to use this list to review your own strengths and weaknesses. Or you could ask someone who is regularly with you in groups and meetings to help you do this. There may be some surprises, not all of them unpleasant.

## Leadership in a learning group

A learning group is not the same thing as a committee. A leader's role is not likely to be the same as that of a chairperson with a detailed agenda.

Considerations before setting up a learning group are:

- Should we appoint a leader (or leaders)?
- What kind of leadership would suit the group? What understanding and skills are needed?
- If there is already a pattern of leadership, do we wish to keep it or change it?
- If we have leaders, what are we asking them to do?
- Can we share the leadership? If so, how will we do that?
- What is the effect of having as leaders clergy, laity, men, women, locals, incomers, experts?
- If there are co-leaders, should one be 'pastoral' (maintenance and individual needs) and the other task-centred (the expert on the subject)? You might, for example, like to complement a flair for seeing things clearly, holding the group to the task and moving the learning on by choosing as a co-leader someone who is more tentative or imaginative or focused on making sure none of the group is left behind in the learning process.

Broadly speaking, if there is more than one leader, it takes more time, more patience and more skill, but it reaches parts a solitary leader can never reach. It also provides training for both, particularly for the less experienced.

### What is needed from the leaders?

Is it true that a teacher/tutor/facilitator is one who . . .

- can answer all the questions which come up?
- is primarily responsible if it is a 'bad' session?
- should be able to bring the group round to a point of agreement if there has been some controversy?
- is responsible for note-taking and keeping records?
- is responsible for seeing that tea/coffee, etc. is available?
- keeps things to time?
- checks what has happened if someone doesn't turn up or fails to complete an assignment?
- remembers a person's birthday or some other personal event?
- makes sure there is an extension lead for the projector?
- does not take things personally when facing conflict?

–   makes sure everyone has a say?

What are the taken-for-granted assumptions about leadership in your context?

As a leader, how would you handle the situation when a person . . .

- has interesting things to say but monopolizes the time?
- goes off at a tangent?
- stops the flow of a presentation by frequently asking questions?
- tries to score points off others in the group including the tutor?
- persistently finds fault with whatever is suggested, albeit in the nicest possible way?
- flatly contradicts what a group member or the tutor has said?
- never joins in?
- persistently comes late or leaves early?
- attacks another group member?
- makes sexist or racist comments?

*Some suggestions from experienced tutors:*

During the session:

'I'll just summarize what X has said and then we'll move on.'

'Please put your questions on hold for a few minutes.'

'Let's have just one comment per person from now on so that everyone has a chance to speak.'

'Is there anyone who hasn't spoken yet who would like to say something?'

'That is an interesting issue but it seems to be different from what this session is about. Maybe over coffee there'll be a chance to talk to someone about it.'

'I agree with you up to a point but after that we must agree to differ. These things are not carved in stone.'

'B, let me summarize what A has just said. It is an area where there is disagreement and it is important that you listen to what is said by the others.'

'The next session starts at Z. We have a lot of work to

cover and time is precious. I would be grateful if everyone could be back in their places by then.'

Outside the session:

- Chat to the non-participant to check if they like being quiet.
- Talk to any 'disruptive' person to see if there is anything to be done to clear up any difficulties. If not, do not keep arguing or defending; otherwise the same person will be having your time and attention outside the group as well as during the session. Often problems have nothing to do with the event: pastoral care may be needed.
- Realize that often people who have been difficult want to find a way out themselves. They may be looking for a graceful face-saving way of changing their attitude.
- Realize too that you are not alone. Groups often have members with very effective ways of dealing with trouble, sometimes with a light touch and with humour and kindness.
- Check the timing and pacing of your programme so that people are not bored or rushed.

# 8

# How Are We Doing?

This chapter has three sections:

A. *Assessment:* what it is and how to do it
B. *Accreditation:* the case for and against
C. *A glossary of terms*

## A. Assessment

Assessment is the process of judging performance on the basis of evidence. All education and training is assessed at some level. It is not an optional extra – we do it as both teachers and learners, looking back over what has happened and making a judgement as to whether or not it was worthwhile. Organizations also need to do it periodically in order to plan for the future. A sample of experience, sometimes over a long period, sometimes short (an exam), is used to draw inferences about our own or someone else's abilities, achievements and aptitudes.

Should assessment of courses or students be formal and public or left to the informal networks of those holding organizational power and influence? This is a very difficult area. Assessment is what it is, nothing more or less. It becomes a problem when it is linked with a lot of other things: accreditation, licensing, authorizing, certification and ordination. Some of these may lead to significant life changes such as access to another course or permission to take on a new ministry. Already we are walking on glass. No process of accreditation or selection is perfect, which is another way of saying it is unjust. We have all been hurt by

110

it in some way on our own behalf or other people's, however much it is run by people of goodwill, prayer, discrimination and experience.

## Why assessment?

It may serve three purposes, two of which are comparatively straightforward.

Firstly, we assess to give the learner (and possibly the tutor) as they go along some idea of how they are doing so that they can realize if they could do something better. This process is often called evaluation.

Secondly, we assess on a slightly larger scale to point out strengths and weaknesses and potential for development.

Thirdly, we sum up, judge achievement, counting what has happened in order to make an overall assessment. This may be linked with some public recognition of achievement: the granting of a certificate, licence or authority to take up a particular role.

## How should it be done?

To be fair and accurate, judgements which are publicly recognized should always be based on specified criteria which apply to certain stated areas. These may point to personal and internal qualities (an empathetic attitude) or external competencies (ability to preach to a certain standard or cover certain points rationally in an essay).

There are many methods:

- observation
- questionnaires
- interviews
- reports
- surveys
- essays
- tests
- examinations
- portfolios
- peers (other students and colleagues who can appraise the person's contribution, skills, knowledge or attitudes

– may be more useful as a learning strategy than as a valid method of assessment)

- self (increasingly used alongside other methods)

## B. *Accreditation*

There is a wide disagreement about the value of accrediting lay people and there are many different policies. It helps to make a distinction between accreditation and authorization, but not much.

But the changes of the last few years mean that the boundary between what the Church accredits and what the national system outside accredits is crumbling. People are passing ever more freely between the two and at least in these early stages are taken by surprise at how seriously what they do for the Church is being taken elsewhere. For example, a farmer's wife who runs a harvest supper in aid of the church fabric will not get a qualification in Christian hospitality . . . But she finds that if she keeps evidence of her activity (receipts, lists, menus, etc.) her competency in catering, budgeting, organizing volunteer help, publicity and handling accounts does count towards a national qualification. So too the churchwarden who has some responsibility for a Grade II listed building.

### The case for accreditation

From the Church's point of view:

- Accreditation makes it easier for the Church to set standards of knowledge and competence in those who exercise particular ministries.
- There would be fewer round pegs in square holes. Accreditation demonstrates that a person can work to the standard required, making selection more accurate.
- Accreditation recognizes and affirms what people are already contributing and identifies further training needs so that they can go on to make an even greater contribution.
- At the moment education and training provision in the Church is patchy and uneven. An accreditation system

which was publicly recognized might help to change that.

From the recipient's point of view:

- Some people would like training and experience (for example, pastoral care undertaken in one part of the country or in one denomination) to be recognized nationally and between denominations so that similar work can be done elsewhere.
- For the many young people who help, for example in children's work and other areas, providing training and qualifications that are nationally recognized could be of real benefit in these days of high unemployment.
- Many of the skills performed by, for example, Sunday School teachers, youth leaders, carers, church administrators, small group leaders, caterers, crèche leaders, flower arrangers, etc., are already covered by current national qualifications. Here is the opportunity for church members (if they wish) to gain qualifications for existing skills under the Accredited Prior Learning (APL) scheme, to improve their skills and gain further qualifications. This may put national qualifications into the hands of people who currently have none.
- There are more and more qualifications based on competency rather than passing exams. The 'fail or pass' attitude is gone, replaced by an assessment *in situ* as often as required until competency is achieved. Measuring the ability to perform the task in question makes achievement possible for a wider range of people.
- A formal accreditation system would regularize what at present happens informally. Voluntary work undertaken for the Church – catering for a church function, youth work, handling large insurance matters – is already being recognized as of sufficient weight to help people to get paid work, to gain access to courses or exemption from modules in some places but not in others. There is similar disparity on completion of, say, an unaccredited Bishop's Certificate Course which may or may not be counted as an A level by some colleges of Higher Education.
- There is a case of accreditation which would ensure co-operation between church colleges of Higher Edu-

cation, theological colleges, Christian training agencies, missionary colleges and so on, so that students can transfer and chart progression routes according to their needs.

## The case against accreditation

From the Church's point of view:

- It could unsettle or exclude those without qualifications or split up the church community into yet more hierarchies.
- There is an important theological issue which has been described as a clash between those educationalists who wish to emphasize the God of justice and order (who may favour accreditation) and those who see a God of profligacy, creativity, play, silence, absence, dispersal and immanence. The former may welcome the development of rigorous, objective methods for defining learning tasks and setting up standardized assessment procedures. The latter may value the amateur, the homespun, the locally grown approach.
- Accreditation can be seen as 'contaminating' the Church with a 1990s tendency to measure and package skills and turn them into a sort of currency. Do performance indicators and contractual (as opposed to convenanted) agreements curtail the energy, imagination and freedom needed to develop schemes of high quality which are exactly tailored to the local context?
- 'Efficiency' is colonizing our entire world. Surely it threatens the very space which sustains us in our daily lives, space where we are free from interference from outside experts and officialdom?
- No accreditation system is perfect and the more formal the system, the harder it is to undo the mistakes.

From the recipient's point of view:

- It leads to false hopes and dashed expectations when the person is not recognized by the Church in the way hoped for.
- We cannot determine beforehand, when entering a situation, where it will lead. God is always moving beyond

what we can imagine. The goal of the educator is not to gather people in and pen them in a defined place but to nurture them and keep them on the move. Accreditation is too cut and dried for something as organic as the spiritual life.

- It may lead to poorer courses. Reliance on technique can mean the adult educator does not have to invent new approaches, state a position and a vision, be critical or even care very much.
- It undermines the notion of democratic partnership between learners and teachers: the joint discovery of knowledge; a relationship of openness and trust.
- Many of the skills and qualities we are seeking to develop elude close definition.

## C. *Glossary*

### Accreditation of Prior Learning (APL)

This is a process of recognizing appropriate learning acquired as a result of life and work experience as well as formal and informal learning. It often means building a portfolio of evidence which is submitted for assessment and hence accreditation. Note it is *learning* which is recognized, not just experience.

What are its benefits?

- It minimizes duplication.
- It improves access for non-traditional candidates.
- It counts existing competencies however obtained.
- It may enhance confidence and a willingness to take on more responsibility.
- It encourages more flexible methods of assessment.

What are the snags?

- It takes time and patience to build up evidence of competency since people usually need help in recognizing and naming their experience. They often underrate themselves.

## Credit Accumulation and Transfer Schemes (CATS)

This is a system of acquiring credits which can be put together to build into a qualification. Instead of studying a particular set course at one place, students can negotiate their own programme of learning from a range of possibilities which suit their circumstances and can be tackled at their pace. So what is learned in one place is recognized by another institution.

What are the benefits?

- It opens up opportunities for students who may not be reached by other means because of their family or work circumstances or the place where they live.
- The learning programme takes account of what they already know, so avoids duplication.
- It is tailor-made for the individual.

What are the snags?

- It does little to promote the vision of the Church as a learning community.
- It can be lonely. The student needs to be highly motivated and to have tutorial support.
- Not everything worth learning can be measured and accredited and these other things may be valued less because of that.

### Competence

In education 'competence' does not mean 'capability' or 'efficiency'. It is a measure of achievement used in many qualifications, even in professional and academic areas. It is found in skills and personal qualities as well as knowledge, understanding and experience necessary for performing a role.

Competence may be divided into conscious and unconscious competence.

Conscious competence comprises those things which you know you can do.

Conscious lack of competence is what you choose to work on to improve your effectiveness.

Unconscious lack of competence is the danger area because you are unaware of the hidden problems.

Unconscious competence is the 'magic' area of which you are as yet unaware. Opening it reveals unsuspected competencies, a process which goes on in portfolio building and in APL.

## Contract

This is an agreement about learning goals drawn up between two or more parties. APL and CATS involve the use of learning contracts. They would include objectives, how to achieve them and how achievement will be demonstrated.

Sometimes it is useful to draw up a learning contract with yourself, setting out aims and objectives with a time scale of achievement. Breaking up what looks like a huge goal into smaller bits which seem possible is often a useful first step.

## Core skills

These are general skills – communication, problem-solving, working with others, etc. – used in a wide range of contexts and contributing to successful performance. There have been various initiatives in Higher Education and elsewhere in recent years to identify and teach them because of their importance, not least in making a link between existing skills and new activities.

## National Vocational Qualifications (NVQs)

These are qualifications based on clear national standards drawn up by the industry/profession to which they relate. They aim to establish common standards at five levels – ranging from routine human activities to substantial personal autonomy and responsibility for the work of others – across a wide range of occupational areas, replacing the old system which was based on numerous awarding bodies each with its own standards.

- They assess competence rather than knowledge by itself and rely on work-based assessments, not examinations.
- They acknowledge past achievements and offer people

without formal training a chance to gain recognition for their existing knowledge and experience.

- They are flexible, being made up of a number of units of competence which allows training to be undertaken as and where opportunities are available.

## Outcomes

These are changes brought about by education and learning and experience. They may be expected or unexpected; be subject-based or personal; may include new knowledge, skills, attitudes and competence. There are outcomes for learners, providers and tutors – and they may be very different. The advantages of thinking about outcomes when embarking on a course are that they encourage clear thinking and emphasize the end result. But it is fair to say that this can be at the cost of missing potentially valuable outcomes because they are not specified.

# 9

## Some Sample Events

This chapter is a series of accounts of how some people tackled particular tasks in ways which are interesting and effective.

Each account was originally written up by the organizer in a slightly longer form for *Adult Network*, details of which are found in the Appendix. In the original text each account includes an evaluation of the event, warts and all. Often much is to be learned from things which did not go according to plan. A taste of the evaluative process is included here.

### 1. What is ministry? (Mike Alexander and Tony Chesterman)

*Aim:* to help those doing a Bishop's Certificate Course to think through its implications for them personally and for the church.

*Method:* Each person was given a worksheet on which to note the implications of the course for

- their personal/family life,
- their vicar/local church,
- their community/neighbourhood,
- their work (paid or unpaid).

People had to opt for a group under one of the four headings. After 40 minutes each group reported back with just three main points.

Over lunch everyone was given a handout with extracts from various documents on lay ministry. Random groups were formed for 45 minutes to discuss two questions using the morning's discussion and the handouts:

- What is ministry?
- What changes in church understanding and structures are needed to fulfil this?

This was followed by a meeting of everyone for reports on ministry (15 minutes) and changes (25 minutes). Everyone was given an envelope and sheet of paper on which to write their understanding of ministry and of the corresponding action needed, both working with others in changing church structure and at a personal level. This was followed by worship and a brief act of dedication/commitment.

***Points from the evaluation:***

(a) The circular shape went well: beginning with individuals – then groups – then the wider church in the extract – then groups again and finally an individual commitment.

(b) Perhaps there should have been more input from the leaders?

(c) It provided some with their first chance to stand back and look at the course and their participation in it.

## 2. Poker . . . or Patience? (Carolyn Henson)

***Aim:*** to help people reflect on a new job undertaken in the Church, sharing their experience with others in a similar situation. Could be adapted for use in many other contexts.

***Method:*** Each group of two or three people is given scissors and an identical set of coloured sheets of A4 card divided into, say, ten sections. Each section has written on it one of the suggestions from a set listed below.

*Card A: Doing my job is sometimes like playing:*

> Happy Families – Snakes and Ladders – poker – ping pong – Patience – a tug of war – Monopoly – blind man's buff – charades – an obstacle race – chess

*Card B: The structures I work in are like:*

a suit of armour – an amoeba – a spider's web – a
corset – a triangle – a climbing frame – a vine –
a chain – a maze – a swimming pool

*Card C: One of the aims is to provide people with:*

a map – a compass – a first-aid kit – a launch pad –
an atlas – a tool kit – a fuel supply – a resting place –
a bunch of keys – a library – a balanced diet – a
community centre – a rule book

*Card D: The way I personally work is like:*

spices – vanilla essence – cornflour – a marinade –
gelatine – olive oil – garlic – sweet and sour sauce –
herbs – lemon juice – HP sauce – salt – cochineal –
yeast

*Card E: To do my job properly I am required to be:*

an organizer – a co-ordinator – an administrator – a
navigator – a general – a diplomat – a theologian –
a juggler – a preacher – a nurse – a politician – a
magician – an artist

### Other possible headings are:

*The resources provided by my organization are like . . .*
*A day's journey in the life of my organization is like a journey
in or on . . .*

The group's task is to cut sections out of each sheet to
make up a hand of, say, twelve small cards. Clearly this
means some discussion and negotiation between the part-
ners working together. When ready the groups display their
hands and talk about their choices in the large group.

***Probable outcomes:*** encouragement, ideas and strategies from
others in similar situations; clarification as to what can and
what cannot be changed; analysis and ordering of priorities;
affirmation of different contributions.

### 3. Apples, pears, blackbirds and maggots (Malcolm Grundy)

*Aim:* to bring together people from four parishes in a new Team Ministry (a definition of Team Ministry had been agreed beforehand and was on display) and to help the new Team Ministry Council with forward planning. About 45 people were involved. The method has already been adapted to other uses.

*Method:* Mixed groups from the four parishes were each given coloured paper shapes which could be placed on a large paper tree on the church hall wall. On the apple shapes they were to write benefits the Team would bring to the churches and the town. On the pears, benefits which would come to individual parishes. On the blackbirds, attacks which could threaten the Team from outside. On the maggots, difficulties which could threaten the team from within.

*Points to note:*

(a) The exercise had novelty value and got people talking and joking, but it needed to be carefully prepared beforehand with the church leadership.

(b) It is useful when a church group is faced with substantial change and fears the unknown. By admitting that there are always some good things lost which could cause trouble (maggots), it is easier to turn to what can be gained from the new (apples and pears).

(c) It sees change in the context of the outside world, not in unrealistic isolation (blackbirds).

(d) The display was later taken round each of the churches to be seen by people who were not there.

(e) What was on the tree could be kept to provide a record of hopes and fears which might be useful in the ups and downs of the new life in the future.

### 4. God's people doing history (Elizabeth Varley)

*Aim:* to see how information is transmitted within a community and so to understand something about the formation of the Gospels. (About 20 people took part, mostly from the same large parish.)

*Method:* People were asked to bring papers, photographs or other records of the ministry of the previous Rector. Three groups were formed and two were placed so that they could just overhear what each was saying, while the third was isolated. Each group was asked to put together in half an hour an outline history of the previous Rector's ministry. Discussion followed and attention was drawn to: the special role of two people who, as it happened, hardly knew him; how discrepancies arose; the difference it had made that two groups could overhear each other; the likely process of producing the Gospels. This first evening ended with free thanskgiving and intercessory prayer which included the previous Rector's ministry.

Homework: everyone chose one Gospel to work on in the light of the discussion.

Second evening: homework was reviewed and findings written up on a flip chart, grouped by Gospel. A short talk followed, on source criticism, form criticism and redaction criticism. There was a quick look at versions, chasing one verse through a wide selection. Prepared sheets invited everyone to answer 'If someone asked you what is meant by "the inspiration of Scripture" what would you say?' Results were pooled and shared. Free prayer time followed.

*Points to note:*

(a) If real and recent history is being dealt with, strong feelings may arise and need to be managed respectfully.

(b) It tackles a difficult area: the group's own experience enabled it to make the jump into biblical criticism.

(c) The short talk on the second evening needs to be accessible to everyone.

(d) The definitions of 'inspiration' exercise needs smaller groups if enough time is available to share ideas afterwards. In any case it produces fresh and rewarding results.

### 5. Two lunchtime sessions for business executives (Krister Ottosson)

*Aim:* to help a small ecumenical group of business men and women reflect on their Christian ministry at work, particularly in a success-orientated society. Time: 50 minutes each lunchtime.

### Method: first session

During soup, cards were handed out with selected biblical verses: Deuteronomy 32.48–50, 52; Hosea 3.1, 2, 4, 5; Luke 7.19–20, 22–23; 2 Timothy 4.3, 4, 6, 7, 9–11; Mark 14.32–37, 39–42.

While sandwiches were eaten, the leader reminded the group of the context in which they had all (previously) said they worked and asked participants to keep this in the back of their minds as each person with a card read it out aloud. The reader was asked to say what thoughts and feelings were provoked. When all the cards were read, there was general discussion.

*Points which came out:* being lonely, powerless, faithful, seeing young people being sucked into the current climate, a 'holding the line' witness.

*Second session a month later:* similar process with different passages: Matthew 27.17, 18, 21–24; Exodus 32.1, 2, 4–6; 1 Kings 21.1–4, 8–10, 16–20.

*Points which came out:* Pilate knew the risks, tried to involve others in the decision, genuinely tried to find a way out but in the end history judges him a coward; so too with Aaron and the golden calf, where some were frightened by being leaderless and others played while the going was good; Naboth's vineyard is a reminder that if you have power you may be tempted to create your own rules and blaming someone else is all too easy; it's natural to want the easy way out; collusions are expensive; be warned if someone is getting you to do their dirty work or if you are tempted to get someone to do yours.

## 6. Warmer welcoming (Richard Bainbridge)

*Aim:* to help PCC members, sidesmen and sideswomen to look at what is involved in welcoming people to Sunday worship in a mixed inner suburban area close to the busy South Circular Road where new people had started to come, many of them black. (About 20 people of mixed age and race took part.)

*Method:* After worship, a welcome by the vicar and introductions, the time was spent in four parts:

- Our own experience of being welcomed
- What we can learn from this in church especially at key points:

  before the service
  the peace
  the administration of communion
  after the service

- Planning in small groups:

  what is good about the way things are done now?
  what could be done to improve them?
  what practical action needs to be taken?

- Closing prayers

*Points to note:*

(a) People said afterwards that the whole congregation should have a chance to do a similar exercise as it was so helpful.
(b) The particular role of the vicar in welcoming may need attention.
(c) There was a practical outcome in that the vicar noticed people were better prepared, more attentive and more aware of each other.
(d) A six-months' review of progress was planned.

## 7. Words! – gospel and culture (Ian Stubbs)

*Aim:* to take a fresh look at the meaning 'religious' words have now.

*Method:* Each person is given a sheet of words and asked to tick a symbol for each one. If the participant is happy to use the word because it is meaningful, a smiling sun; if the word is used sometimes but with caution, a fragile egg; if the word is a dead word with little meaning, a skull.

The list included these words:

TRINITY, SACRED, GRACE, SIN, SACRIFICE, PEACE, KING, INCARNATION, REPENTANCE, CREATOR, LORD, CONFESSION, MAKER, HOLY, GOD, ALMIGHTY, SAVIOUR, CROSS, DEVIL, HELL, KINGDOM, LOVE, SPIRIT, ASCENSION, GHOST, FATHER, BLESSED, MIRACLE, SACRAMENT, RIGHTEOUSNESS.

After completing the exercise in silence, a discussion raised these points:

- why people are unhappy with some words;
- the changing nature of religious language;
- the way Christians become 'multilingual', only using certain words in certain contexts lest they be misunderstood;
- the need to design new metaphors for speaking of God;
- what this means for those wanting to share the gospel.

## 8. New on the scene (Anne Faulkner)

*Aim:* to introduce newcomers to the complexities of agenda-building and minute-taking. (16 people took part.) (Originally intended for those newly appointed as Mothers' Union Diocesan Officers.)

*Method:* There were three groups, each with an identical set of cards on which were written possible agenda items for a 90-minute committee meeting (some were left blank for participants' suggestions). Too many items were on offer so that people had to select.

In 30 minutes, each group had to decide

- the purpose of the committee being planned;
- which items to include in what order;
- the approximate time each would take.

Then

> Group 1 became the host group staying where it was.
> Group 2 became the visiting group which went to
>   Group 1.
> Group 3 became the scribe group taking minutes.

Group 1 had to explain and justify its choice of agenda items under questioning from Group 2, while Group 3 silently took the minutes of what was happening. The groups changed roles so they had a chance to experience all three tasks and this merry-go-round took 45 minutes.

*Points from the evaluation:*

(a)  A variety of methods was used 'to take minutes' and this provoked thinking about the purpose of minutes and the usefulness of different styles.

(b)  It challenged the items which just get put on the agenda without thinking: 'Do we need to read reports at every meeting?' 'Why not have AOB at the beginning?'

(c)  It gave participants a chance to practise writing minutes and then think about their usefulness, knowing that other people were going to do it too.

(d)  Had there been time it might have been possible to get the groups to write their own handout on:
- criteria for agenda building
- timing an agenda
- the difference between minutes and notes
- the purpose of minutes

and this might have consolidated the learning and given participants something to take home and keep for future reference.

### 9. Training the trainers (Keith Lamdin)

*Aim:* to provide an opportunity for 14 people to practise designing a day which held together theology and insights from the human sciences.

*Method:* Introductions followed by time in silence to sort out what issues participants were currently thinking about, followed by an invitation to write their thoughts and feelings (still in silence) on flip-chart paper on the wall. In the discussion that followed three themes (and groups) were identified: Hope and Hopelessness, Angry Christians, and Finding our Way. For three hours (including lunch) each group produced an aim in one sentence and a design for a training day, honouring both the experience of the people of God in the Bible and Church history *and* their own experience.

Each group presented its design. After buzz groups when what was liked and disliked was shared, each person chose the design personally preferred and then the design which would be most useful in a particular context (which may or may not be the same).

### Points from the evaluation:

(a)   Starting with issues which people chose themselves and knew to be relevant to their work meant that there were a lot of ideas and creativity at the beginning.

(b)   The design teams worked well because people were working with others who also had chosen the topic.

(c)   Connections between experience, the Bible and planning action were made but the contribution which theology could have made in the three chosen areas was not properly explored. It probably needed another session.

# Appendix

# Useful Organizations and Further Reading

**Ecumenical organizations**

Adult Network
An association for anyone with an interest in adult Christian education and training. Publishes news of resources (*Adult Network*), runs conferences, supports local networks. Contact Adult Education Department, Board of Education, Great Smith Street, London SW1P 3NZ
ACATE (Association of Centres of Theological Education)
Publishes a *Journal* and *Newsletter*, organizes conferences and working groups. Contact David Goodbourn, St Colm's Centre, 20 Inverleith Terrace, Edinburgh EH3 5NS
TEEF (Theological Education by Extension Forum)
For people involved in writing, managing and supporting distance learning schemes. Contact Revd Ambrose Mason, Oak Hill Theological College, Southgate, London N14 4PS
CSTC (Christian Service Training Council)
Lists resources and encourages working relationships between colleges, churches, missions, etc. Voting members of Council expected to assent to Evangelical Alliance basis of faith. Contact Adrian West, 4 Woodbank Close, Wistaston, Crewe, Cheshire CW2 6SD

**Further reading**

*Chapter 1*

*All Are Called: Towards a theology of the laity* (essays published by General Synod, 1985; now out of print)
*Called to be Adult Disciples* (a follow-up booklet published by

General Synod, 1987; available from the Adult Education Department, Church House)
*What Prevents Christian Adults from Learning?*, Professor John Hull, University of Birmingham (Trinity Press International, 1991)

## Chapter 2

*Christian Education and Training for the 21st Century: What are your priorities?* (General Synod Misc. 389, 1992; available from Church House Bookshop; briefly sets out optional strategies)
*Models of Adult Religious Education Practice*, R. E. Y. Wickett (Religious Education Press, Birmingham, Alabama, 1991)
*Adult Way to Faith*, Peter Ball (Mowbray, 1992; practical handbook on the Adult Catechumenate movement)
*Empowerment through Experiential Learning: Explorations of good practice* (Kogan Page, 1992; papers from the International Conference on Experiential Learning held at the University of Surrey, including 'Learner experience: a rich resource for training' by Dr Tony Saddington (University of Cape Town), which forms the basis of this chapter)
*Freedom to Learn*, Carl Rogers (Merrill, 1969)
*Pedagogy of the Oppressed*, Paulo Freire (Penguin, 1972)
*Using Experience for Learning*, ed. D. Boud, R. Cohen and D. Walker (Open University, 1993)

## Chapter 3

*Making Adult Disciples*, Anton Baumohl (Scripture Union, 1986)
*Culture and Processes of Adult Learning*, ed. Mary Thorpe, Richard Edwards and Ann Hanson and *Adult Learners, Education and Training*, ed. Richard Edwards, Sandy Sieminski and David Zeldin (both Open University, 1993; readers for the OU course Learning Through Life (EH266))
*The Open Learning Handbook: Selecting, designing and supporting open learning materials*, Phil Race (Kogan Page, 1989)
*Personal and Career Development: A portfolio approach* (Open University, 1993; OU course (E530) available for students to use on their own or as an accredited tutor-supported course)

## Chapter 4

Learning Styles manuals and workshops: Dr P. Honey, Ardingley House, 10 Linden Avenue, Maidenhead, Berkshire SL6 6HB

*Getting Started with the Learning Styles Software*, C. Jackson and J. Morris (Corporate Assessment Network Ltd, 44 Sheen Lane, East Sheen, London SW14 8LG, 1993)

'Towards an applied theory of experiential learning', D. A. Kolb and R. Frey in *Theories of Group Processes*, ed. C. L. Cooper (Wiley, 1975)

*People Types and Tiger Stripes: A practical guide to learning styles*, Gordon Lawrence (Centre for Applications of Psychological Types, Gainesville, Florida, 1989; based on ideas from Carl Jung and Isabel Briggs Myers)

## Chapter 5

*Transforming Bible Study: A leader's guide*, Walter Wink (reprinted Mowbray and Abingdon Press, 1990)

*Through the Eyes of a Woman: Bible studies*, Wendy Robins (World YMCA, 1986)

*Using Video in Training and Education*, Ashley Pinnington (McGraw-Hill Training Series, 1992)

*Active Training: A handbook of techniques, designs, case examples and tips*, M. Silberman (Lexington Books, 1990)

*Lecturing and Explaining*, George Brown (Methuen, 1987)

*Reflection: Turning experience into learning*, D. Boud, R. Keogh and D. Walker (Kogan Page, 1985)

*Catching Fire*, Elizabeth Varley (Bible Society, 1993)

## Chapter 7

*Understanding Groups: A study course of five sessions, each of two hours*, Paul Bates and Lois Smith on behalf of the St Albans Diocesan Board of Ministry (available from The Taleteller, 5 Little Cloister, Westminster Abbey, London SW1 3PA; 30 A4 pages)

*Once upon a Group . . .*, Michael Kindred (published for Southwell Diocesan Board of Education and available from Michael Kindred, 20 Dover Street, Southwell, Notts NG2 0EZ, 118 A5 pages)

*Working Together: A handbook for groups* (The Catholic Fund for Overseas Development (CAFOD), the Catholic Institute for International Relations, Pax Christi and the Scottish Catholic International Aid Fund, 1986; primarily for groups with a particular concern for justice and peace issues; 30 A4 pages)

*A Health Guide for Small Groups: A training manual for those who lead or belong to small groups, for individuals or group,* Anton Baumohl (Small Group Resources, 48 Peterborough Road, London SW6 3EB; primarily for Bible study groups; (sessions of $1\frac{1}{2}$ hours))

*Chapter 8*

*Measuring Performance in the Education of Adults,* Bob Powell (NIACE, 1991)

**Other useful addresses**

National Council for Vocational Qualifications
222 Euston Road, London NW1 2BZ

Open University
Walton Hall
Milton Keynes MK7 6AA
Telephone: 0908 274066

National Institute of Adult Continuing Education
19b De Montfort Street
Leicester LE1 7GE
Telephone: 0533 551451